621.395

OPERATIONAL AMPLIFIER
USER'S HANDBOOK

SIXT

D1512753

below

Other Titles of Interest

OPERATIONAL AMPLIFIER
USER'S HANDBOOK

by

R. A. PENFOLD

BERNARD BABANI (publishing) LTD
THE GRAMPIANS
SHEPHERDS BUSH ROAD
LONDON W6 7NF
ENGLAND

Please Note

Although every care has been taken with the production of this book to ensure that any projects, designs, modifications and/or programs, etc., contained herewith, operate in a correct and safe manner and also that all components specified are normally available in Great Britain, the Publishers and Author do not accept responsibility in any way for the failure, including fault in design, of any project, design, modification or program to work correctly or to cause damage to any other equipment that it may be connected to or used in conjunction with, or in respect of any other damage or injury that may be so caused, nor do the Publishers accept responsibility in any way for the failure to obtain specified components.

Notice is also given that if equipment that is still under warranty is modified in any way or used or connected with home-built equipment then that warranty may be void.

© 1994 BERNARD BABANI (publishing) LTD

First Published — January 1994

British Library Cataloguing in Publication Data
Penfold, R. A.
  Operational Amplifier User's Handbook
  I. Title
  621.3815

  ISBN 0 85934 335 9

Printed and Bound in Great Britain by Cox & Wyman Ltd, Reading

Preface

Designers of electronic components are often accused of producing clever components in the hope that someone will then come up with a few practical applications for the new wonder devices. This was certainly not the case with operational amplifier integrated circuits, which were designed specifically for one purpose. They were designed to operate as precision d.c. amplifiers for use in analogue computers. In a way though, operational amplifiers did suffer from the "cart before the horse" syndrome. Circuit designers soon found all manner of uses for operational amplifiers, and were soon utilizing this new type of amplifier in vast numbers. The standard 741C has probably been made in larger numbers than any other semiconductor component.

Many of the early operational amplifiers had quite respectable levels of performance. Some are still in common use and, unlike most semiconductors of that era, are still available as "off the shelf" items. However, as technology improved, new devices were steadily introduced. These offer various improvements on the standard 741C, such as lower audio noise, greater precision in d.c. applications, and wider bandwidth. A huge range of operational amplifiers is now available. Finding the right device for a given application can be a confusing process.

In this book the properties and applications of modern operational amplifiers are discussed. In Chapter 1 the standard operational amplifier "building blocks" are covered, with attention being paid to the improvements in performance that are available using modern devices. Chapter 2 covers practical applications using modern operational amplifiers, such as very low noise, precision d.c., high output current, and wide bandwidth types.

R. A. Penfold

Contents

Chapter 2 (Continued)

Chapter 1

OPERATIONAL AMPLIFIER PARAMETERS

Integrated circuit operational amplifiers are extremely popular devices, and have been since the early days of integrated circuits. While the popularity of many types of semiconductor has waned in recent years, operational amplifiers seem to have maintained their position. In fact they seem to be used more now than ever before. The range of available devices is now vast. Most of the "golden oldies" are still readily available, and in some cases are still in large scale production. In addition to these, several generations of improved devices are to be found in most electronic components catalogues.

The enduring popularity of operational amplifiers is perhaps a little surprising, since they were originally designed for a rather specialised purpose. They were made for use in analogue computers where they were used to perform mathematical operations, and it was from this that the name "operational amplifier" was derived. The world of computing is now dominated by digital electronics, and analogue computers are now totally obsolete. However, operational amplifiers proved to be useful in a wide range of applications. Analogue computers have become relics of the past, but operational amplifiers are now used in more applications than ever before.

An operational amplifier is really just a form of d.c. amplifier, and as such it has obvious applications in many fields of electronics. As a couple of examples, d.c. amplifiers are much used in electronic test equipment, and most types of electronic sensing/measurement. Although operational amplifiers were designed to provide d.c. amplification, with suitable biasing most modern devices will work perfectly well as a.c. amplifiers.

Apart from a few specialised devices, most operational amplifiers are not suitable for use at high frequencies. Most types will work well at audio frequencies though. In fact many of the devices currently on sale are specifically designed for use in high quality audio applications. The noise and distortion performance of these audio operational amplifiers rivals specialist audio preamplifier chips, and in some cases easily surpasses most of the audio preamplifier chips. Because of their high performance and versatility, audio operational amplifiers seem to be more popular than audio preamplifier chips.

Although the original integrated circuit operational amplifiers worked well enough in their primary role, they were less well suited to many other potential applications. This has led to the development of numerous improved devices, which give superior performance in one or more respects when compared to the standard devices. In this chapter we will consider the basic operation of the more common operational amplifier circuit blocks, paying particular attention to the ways in which modern operational amplifiers can give enhanced performance.

In Theory

An operational amplifier is a form of differential amplifier, and the output voltage is governed by the voltage difference across the two input terminals. The inputs are the inverting (−) and non-inverting (+) types. Taking the non-inverting input to a higher potential than the inverting input results in a positive output voltage. Taking the inverting input to the higher voltage results in the output going negative. A theoretically perfect operational amplifier has an infinite voltage gain, but obviously no practical device can achieve this. The voltage gains of most operational amplifiers are very high though, and the standard 741C for instance, has a typical voltage gain of 106dB (200,000 times). A few types have higher voltage gains, but for most practical purposes there is no advantage in having a voltage gain of more than about 100dB (100,000 times). Consequently, this is one respect in which modern operational amplifiers offer no improvement over earlier types.

In their original application there was no real need for operational amplifiers to offer wide bandwidths. There was usually no point in striving to produce an analogue computer that would produce an answer in a fraction of a microsecond, because it would then take someone a second or two to actually read the answer to the computation. Even today, there are still many d.c. applications that do not require amplifiers having wide bandwidths. On the other hand, with many operational amplifiers now being used in audio and other a.c. applications, the bandwidths of operational amplifiers is often of crucial importance.

Many beginners run into difficulties when using operational amplifiers as they fail to take into account their bandwidths. Although they have high d.c. voltage gains, the gain starts to roll-off at what is in many cases a frequency of just a few hertz. In operational amplifier data sheets the gain bandwidth product is the parameter which enables the voltage gain to be determined for any given frequency.

The standard 741C has a gain bandwidth product of 1MHz, which means that its voltage gain falls to unity at a frequency of 1MHz. The gain rises at 6dB per octave below this frequency (i.e. the voltage gain doubles each time the input frequency is halved). This continues until the full voltage gain of 200,000 times is reached. Except at low frequencies where the full voltage gain is achieved, the voltage gain is equal to the gain bandwidth product divided by the input frequency. In this case the gain bandwidth product is 1MHz (1,000,000Hz), so dividing 1,000,000 by the input frequency (in hertz) gives the voltage gain at that input frequency. For instance, at a frequency of 5kHz (5000Hz), the voltage gain is only 200 times (1,000,000/5000 = 200).

Clearly it is not possible to obtain high voltage gains at audio frequencies using a 741C. The upper limit of the audio range is generally accepted as 20kHz, and at this frequency a 741C offers a voltage gain of just 50 times (34dB). On the face of it, operational amplifiers are totally unsuitable for use as audio amplifiers due to the 6dB per octave roll-off across the full audio range. In reality this is not a problem, as the voltage gain of a practical amplifier is controlled by a negative feedback loop. The innate voltage gain of an operational amplifier is its "open loop" voltage gain. The voltage gain of the amplifier circuit as a whole is the "closed loop" voltage gain.

Inverting Amplifier

There are two basic amplifying configurations for operational amplifiers, which are the inverting and non-inverting varieties.

3

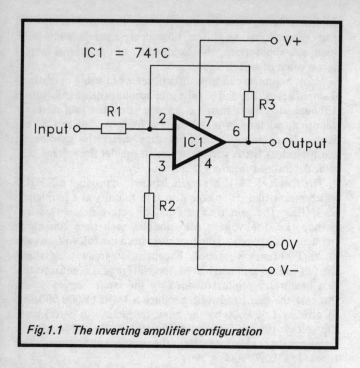

Fig.1.1 The inverting amplifier configuration

As these names suggest, with the inverting type the input and output signals are 180 degrees out-of-phase, whereas they are in-phase for a non-inverting amplifier. The two basic configurations are shown in Figures 1.1 (inverting) and 1.2 (non-inverting). These are d.c. amplifier circuits which can handle positive and negative input voltages, and which can provide output signals of either polarity. They require dual balanced supplies with a central 0 volt earth rail.

R1 and R3 form the negative feedback network. The closed loop voltage gain of the inverting amplifier is equal to R3 divided by R1, and the input resistance is equal to the value of R1. One reason for the popularity of operational amplifiers is the ease with which the voltage gain and input resistance (or impedance for an a.c. amplifier) can be set. If an input resistance of 10k and a voltage gain of 10 times (20dB) were required, R1 would obviously be given a value of

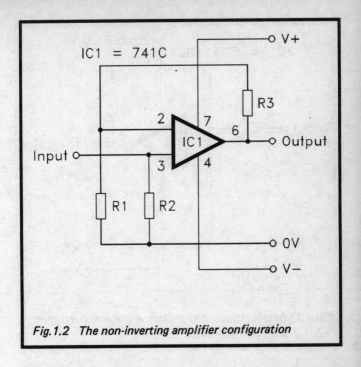

Fig.1.2 The non-inverting amplifier configuration

10k. R3 would need to have a value ten times higher, or 100k in other words.

In theory, R2 is not necessary, and the non-inverting input of IC1 (pin 3) could be connected direct to the 0 volt supply rail. In practice this can result in errors at the output due to the bias currents that flow into the inputs of IC1, and the voltages that this produces across the feedback resistors. The purpose of R2 is to counteract the effect of the input currents. The correct value for R2 is equal to R1 × R3/(R1 + R3). With our example values of 10k and 100k for R1 and R3, this equals 9.09 (1000k/110k = 9.09k). In practice the nearest preferred value of 9k1 would be used.

In practical applications the output errors caused by the input currents are often too small to be of significance. Also, many modern operational amplifiers have some form of field effect transistor (f.e.t.) input stage. These draw such low

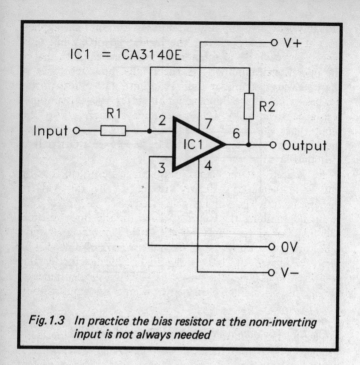

Fig. 1.3 In practice the bias resistor at the non-inverting input is not always needed

input currents that they are totally insignificant, even if high value feedback resistors are used. R2 then becomes unnecessary, and can then be replaced by a shorting link (Figure 1.3).

Non-Inverting Amplifier

The mathematics of the non-inverting amplifier are nearly as straightforward as those of the inverting type. R2 biases the non-inverting input to the 0 volt supply rail, and with this configuration it can not simply be replaced with a shorting link. This is due to the fact that the input signal is applied to the non-inverting input. The purpose of R2 is to set the required input resistance, and it is simply given a value which is equal to the required input resistance.

In some cases R2 is not needed. If the input of the amplifier will always be connected to a signal source (a previous amplifier stage in the circuit for instance), then R2 will probably not serve any useful purpose. Also, in some applications it is necessary to have the highest possible input resistance. Omitting R2 gives an input resistance equal to that of the operational amplifier. In theory the input resistance of the operational amplifier itself is infinite. For "real world" devices which have bipolar input stages the actual input resistance is normally a few megohms or more. For f.e.t. input types the input resistance is usually a few thousand megohms or more, and in some cases is in excess of a million megohms!

R1 and R3 set the closed loop voltage gain of the circuit, but the mathematics is slightly different to that for an inverting amplifier. The voltage gain is equal to $(R1 + R3)/R1$. When determining the correct values for the three resistors the first task is to simply set R2 at the desired input resistance. For the sake of this example we will assume that an input resistance of 10k is required. Ideally the parallel resistance of R1 and R3 should be equal to the resistance of R2, as this will minimise any errors due to the input currents of IC1.

For medium to high voltage gains it is usually acceptable to give R1 the same value as R2. This does not give perfectly balanced results, but the relatively high value of R3 will not upset the biasing to any great extent. For a voltage gain of 20 times for instance, good results would be produced using a value of 10k for R1, and 190k for R3. The value of R3 is equal to R1 multiplied by one less than the required voltage gain (10k × 19 = 190k). For low voltage gains the effect of R3 has to be taken into account. A voltage gain of two times would require a value of 20k for both R1 and R3. This gives the correct voltage gain, and 20k plus 20k in parallel gives a resistance of 10k (exactly equal to the value of R2).

The circuit of Figure 1.2 gives correct biasing with no input signal applied to the circuit. In a practical application the input of the circuit will often be fed from a low output impedance signal source. It would then be correct to feed the input signal to the non-inverting input of IC1 via R2, rather than having R2 provide biasing to the 0 volt supply rail.

In many practical applications it is not necessary to balance the resistance of R1 and R3 to that of R2. Any biasing errors produced may simply be too small to be of any consequence in a non-critical application, or the use of low input current operational amplifiers might make the biasing highly accurate even without any balancing. In such cases the values of R1 and R3 should be such that R3 is not so low in value that the output of the amplifier is heavily loaded by the feedback network. Although a theoretical operational amplifier has an output impedance of zero ohms and can provide unlimited output current, most practical devices can only provide output currents of up to a few milliamps. The series resistance through R1 and R3 should be no less than a few kilohms, and ideally would be much higher at around 50k.

On the other hand, very high values are also undesirable. In theory there is no problem if resistor values of many megohms are used. This is due to the fact that a theoretical operational amplifier does not have any input capacitance, and there are no stray capacitances anywhere in the theoretical circuit. In reality these capacitances do exist, and can produce problems with instability. They can also produce irregularities in the frequency response of the amplifier, although this is not likely to be of any real importance in true d.c. applications. It can be a major problem with audio amplifiers though, especially when using f.e.t input devices (which have relatively high input capacitances). A resistance through the feedback network of between 10k and 100k should provide good results.

Voltage Followers

Operational amplifiers are often used as voltage followers. This is a non-inverting amplifier which has unity voltage gain, but has a high input impedance and a low output impedance. In other words it acts as a buffer amplifier, rather like a bipolar transistor used as an emitter follower. The voltage follower configuration is shown in Figure 1.4. R1 sets the required input resistance (where appropriate), and no negative feedback network is needed. The inverting input simply connects direct to the output of IC1.

Offset Null

Even when carefully designed bias circuits are used,

8

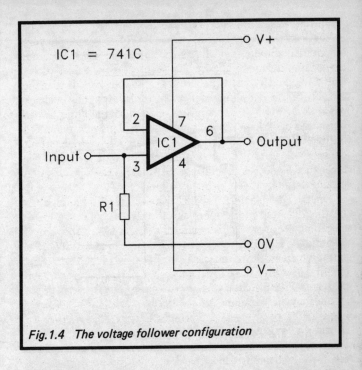

Fig.1.4 The voltage follower configuration

operational amplifiers can still produce output voltage errors. This problem is most likely to occur when very high voltage gains are involved. A very small error at the inputs can become a huge error at the output, because the input error will be amplified by the closed loop gain of the amplifier. There are several potential causes of an offset voltage at the output, but the major cause is usually a slight lack of balance in the operational amplifier itself. In critical applications it is best to use a high quality instrumentation grade operational amplifier that is guaranteed to offer a high degree of accuracy, with minimal offsets. These tend to be very much more expensive than the standard devices, but their ease of use more than justifies the extra cost.

The alternative is to use an offset null control. Figure 1.5 shows the offset null control for the 741C, or any device which is fully compatible with the 741C. Note that many

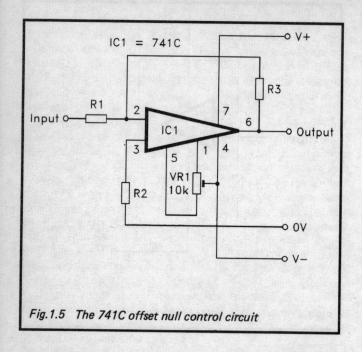

Fig.1.5 The 741C offset null control circuit

operational amplifiers are not fully compatible with the 741C, and have a different offset null arrangement. Ideally VR1 should be a multi-turn preset potentiometer, but it is usually possible to obtain good results with an ordinary type if it is adjusted very carefully. VR1 is simply adjusted for zero output voltage with no input signal applied to the circuit.

It is only fair to point out that offset null controls are not popular with circuit designers. They are believed by many circuit designers to have a drift problem, with frequent readjustment being necessary. My experience would seem to bear out this reputation for drift problems, and it would seem to be more practical to have the offset null potentiometer as a front panel control rather than a preset potentiometer tucked away inside the equipment. Where possible it is better to use a circuit that does not need an offset null control, even if this means using a much more expensive operational amplifier.

10

Single Supply

Conventionally, operational amplifiers operate from dual balanced supply rails with a central 0 volt earth rail. This is not strictly necessary, and it is perfectly possible to have d.c. amplifiers which operate from a single supply rail. The only proviso is that with single supply operation it is not possible to have negative output voltages. In most modern applications of operational amplifiers this restriction is of no practical importance.

Although single supply operation is perfectly feasible, it is not possible using the 741C and most other operational amplifiers. This is due to the fact that these devices were only designed for operation on dual supplies, and they do not have suitable characteristics for single supply use. The main requirements for operation on one supply are inputs and outputs that can operate at voltages right down to the 0 volt supply rail. Remember that with just the one supply, the negative supply pin of the operational amplifier connects to the 0 volt supply rail. Under quiescent conditions the output and both inputs will be at 0 volts. The 741C and many other operational amplifiers have n.p.n. bipolar input transistors used in circuits which prevent them from operating with input voltages of less than about 2 volts above the negative supply pin. Similarly, the output stages can not provide voltages of less than about this same figure.

Some operational amplifiers are designed for operation on a single supply, but it should be noted that these devices are also perfectly suitable for conventional dual supply use. The input stages are based on either field effect transistors or bipolar p.n.p. transistors so that they will operate properly at potentials right down to the 0 volt supply rail. The output stages utilize CMOS technology or bipolar p.n.p. transistors used in class A. Again, this permits operation at potentials right down to the 0 volt supply rail. Probably the best known of these single supply operational amplifiers is the CA3140E, which uses a PMOS input stage and a class A p.n.p. output stage. Other devices which are suitable for single supply operation include the CA3240E (the dual version of the CA3140E), the CA3130E (a CMOS type), the LM358N and the LM324N (which are respectively dual and quad bipolar

11

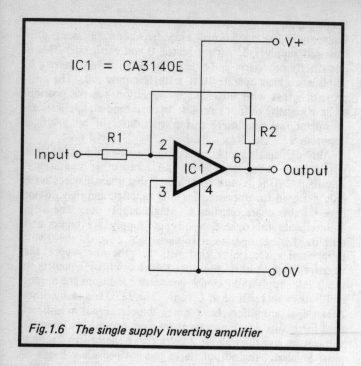

Fig. 1.6 The single supply inverting amplifier

types).

Figures 1.6 and 1.7 respectively show the single supply versions of the inverting and non-inverting circuits. These are really just the same as the dual supply versions, but the negative supply pin connects to the 0 volt supply rail instead of the absent negative supply rail. Note that the input of the non-inverting circuit must always be positive of the 0 volt supply rail, so that a positive output voltage is produced. Similarly, the input to the inverting circuit must always be a negative signal, so that a positive output voltage is produced.

Differential Amplifier

An operational amplifier is, as explained previously, a differential amplifier which amplifies the voltage difference across its two inputs. Some practical applications require a differential amplifier, but simply applying the input signals direct to

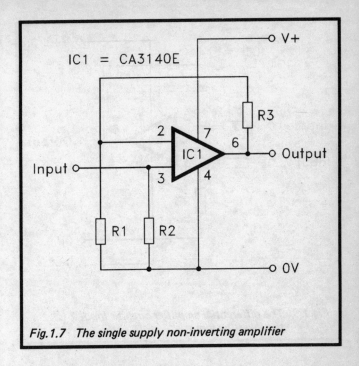

Fig.1.7 The single supply non-inverting amplifier

an operational amplifier will not usually provide the desired result. Negative feedback must be used to give the desired closed loop gain, much as it is for simple voltage amplifiers based on operational amplifiers. Figure 1.8 shows the configuration for a differential amplifier.

Input 1 is the inverting input, and a positive input here sends the output more negative. R1 and R4 are the negative feedback network which sets the voltage gain at this input in standard inverting amplifier fashion. This negative feedback network also sets the voltage gain at input 2, which is the non-inverting input. A positive voltage at this input therefore sends the output more positive. There is a slight problem in that R1 and R4 set the voltage gain at input 2 one higher than the voltage gain at input 1. This is simply due to the slightly different mathematics for inverting and non-inverting mode voltage gains, as explained previously. In practical applications

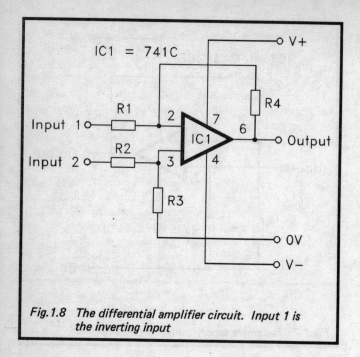

Fig. 1.8 The differential amplifier circuit. Input 1 is the inverting input

this imbalance in the voltage gains of the two inputs might be of no importance. However, where necessary an input resistor at the non-inverting input (R2) can be used to provide some attenuation in order to balance the gains.

There are two main applications for differential input stages. One is where noise picked up in the input wiring must be minimised. Instead of applying the input signal from earth to the input of a simple voltage amplifier, it is applied across the two inputs of a differential amplifier. The point of this is that any noise picked up at one input will cancel out the noise picked up at the other input. It is assumed here that the two noise signals will be identical, and in practice it is unlikely that there will be any significant difference between them. The cancelling will only be perfect if the input sensitivities at the two inputs are identical. In a "real world" differential amplifier R2 is often a preset resistor so that the circuit can be adjusted for optimum noise cancelling. Input stages of this type are called "balanced line" preamplifiers, and they are mainly used in applications where very low signal levels are involved. For optimum results a very low noise instrumentation grade operational amplifier should be used.

The other main application is where two in-phase signals must be mixed together, but in such a way that they cancel each other out rather than being added together. Circuits of this type are quite often needed in practical applications.

Summing Up

Figure 1.9 shows the basic circuit for a summing mode mixer. This provides the opposite action to a differential amplifier. The latter effectively subtracts one input signal from the other. Inputs of the same polarity cancel each other out, while voltages of the opposite polarity are added together. A summing mode mixer is a straightforward adding circuit.

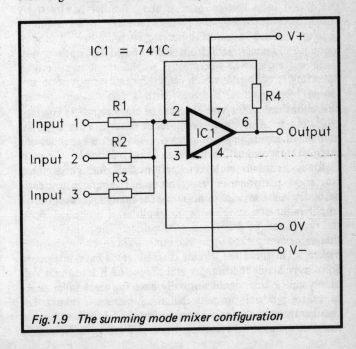

Fig.1.9 The summing mode mixer configuration

Inputs of the same polarity add together, while those of the opposite polarity tend to cancel one another out. However, it should be noted that this type of circuit is based on the inverting amplifier mode, and the output is of the opposite polarity to the total input signal.

The circuit is really just a standard inverting mode amplifier, but there are several inputs with an input resistor for each one. The input resistance at each input is equal to the value of the input resistor, and the voltage gain is equal to the value of R4 divided by the input resistor's value. In practical summing mode mixer circuits the input resistors are usually equal in value. However, this is not essential, and different values can be used in order to provide a different input resistance and voltage gain at each input.

Although the circuit of Figure 1.9 has three inputs, the circuit can (in theory) have any desired number of inputs. A point that is often overlooked with this type of circuit is that the closed loop voltage gain of the amplifier is effectively equal to R4 divided by the parallel resistance of all the input resistors. Using a lot of inputs, even with only a modest amount of voltage gain from each one to the output, puts quite a strain on the operational amplifier. It is effectively operating at high gain, which gives increased output noise, low closed loop bandwidth, etc. With a theoretically perfect operational amplifier you can have as many inputs as you like, but using a "real world" component there is a limit on the number of inputs that can be used. This limit is dependent on many factors though, and it is not easily defined. The main factor is the minimum level of performance that is acceptable. For good performance using numerous inputs it is clearly necessary to use a low noise, wide bandwidth operational amplifier.

Integrator

Figure 1.10 shows the circuit diagram for a basic integrator. R2 simply biases the non-inverting input of IC1 to the 0 Volt supply rail. This would normally have the same value as R1 so as to produce properly balanced biasing. In practical circuits though, the non-inverting input of IC1 is often just wired direct to the 0 volt supply rail, and doing this is unlikely

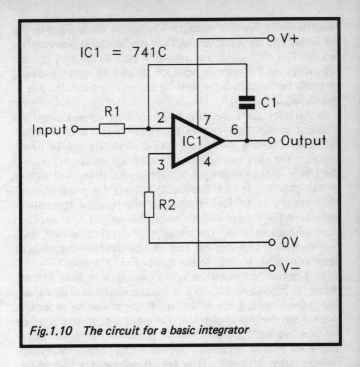

Fig.1.10 *The circuit for a basic integrator*

to produce any significant output errors.

Taking the input of the circuit to a positive potential results in the output going negative at a constant rate. What actually happens is that a charge current flows into C1 in order to counteract the input current through R1. As C1 charges up, the output has to go more and more negative in order to maintain a constant charge current that is equal and opposite to the input current through R1. This process continues until the output goes fully negative. A negative input voltage has much the same effect, but it produces a positive output voltage that rises at a constant rate.

An integrator is used in applications where the output voltage must be a measure of both the input level and the amount of time that the input signal is present. It should be noted here that the rate at which the output voltage rises is dependent on the input voltage as well as the amount of time that the input signal is present. The higher the input voltage, the higher the input current, and the greater the charge current fed to C1. Of course, the rate at which C1 charges is also dependent on the time constant of C1 and R1, and the values of these two components must be carefully selected to suit a given application.

Integrators are only used in a relatively limited range of practical applications, but an integrator is still a very useful electronic building block, and one that should not be overlooked. They are mainly used in waveform generators, where the linear change in output voltage makes them well suited to the production of triangular and linear ramp waveforms. They are also useful for certain types of measuring equipment, such as a photographic flash meter. Here the final reading must take into account the intensity of the flash of light, and its duration. This can be achieved by feeding the output signal from a photodiode to the input of an integrator.

In practical circuits it is often necessary to have a reset circuit to discharge C1 once a reading has been taken, so that a fresh reading can be taken. It might also be necessary to have an electronic switch at the input which only couples the input signal to the integrator at the correct time. Although simple in theory, practical circuits using integrators often become rather involved. They are often based on f.e.t. input operational amplifiers which have extremely high input resistances. This enables readings to be held for a reasonable length of time. Using a 741C is likely to result in the charge on C1 decaying quite rapidly once the input signal has been removed.

Differentiator

A differentiator is one of the less well known types of circuit, and I suppose that it is not a type of circuit that is used a great deal in "real world" applications. Figure 1.11 shows the circuit for a differentiator. This is basically the same as for an integrator, but the timing resistor and capacitor (C1 and R2) have been swapped over. The input current is proportional to the rate at which the input voltage changes. The output produces a current flow through R2 that will balance the input current. Consequently, a slowly changing input

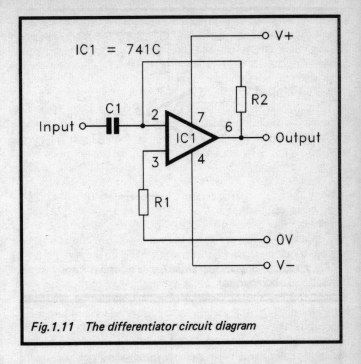

Fig.1.11   The differentiator circuit diagram

voltage produces a small output voltage, and a rapidly changing input signal produces a large output voltage. Bear in mind that this is another variation on the basic inverting amplifier circuit, and that the output voltage is therefore of the opposite polarity to the input signal.

Voltage Comparator
Operational amplifiers are frequently used as voltage comparators. In its most basic form, a voltage comparator can consist of nothing more than the operational amplifier itself (Figure 1.12).   All a voltage comparator does is to provide a fully positive or fully negative output, depending on the relative amplitudes of two input voltages. If the non-inverting input is at the higher voltage the output goes positive — if the inverting input is at the higher voltage the output goes negative.

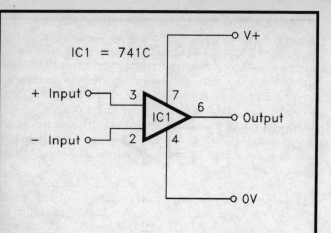

Fig. 1.12 An operational amplifier as a basic voltage comparator

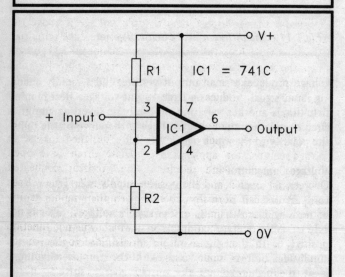

Fig. 1.13 A voltage comparator having a built-in reference voltage

There is a slight flaw in this type of circuit in that an operational amplifier is strictly speaking an amplifier, not a true comparator. With the input voltages very closely matched it is possible that the output will take up an intermediate level, rather than going fully positive or negative. In practice it is very difficult to obtain intermediate output levels due to the very high d.c. voltage gain of an operational amplifier. Even a difference of just a tenth of a millivolt is sufficient to send the output voltage fully one way or the other. As we shall see later, it is possible to ensure that intermediate output voltages can never be produced.

In most practical applications of voltage comparators one input voltage is a reference level, and the other is a varying voltage from something like a sensor. One input is then fed from the supply lines via a potential divider, and the other input is fed with the input signal, as in Figure 1.13. The values of R1 and R2 are selected to produce the required reference voltage, or in a critical application a highly stable reference voltage generator would be used instead. The input voltage is applied to the non-inverting input of IC1, and the output therefore goes high if input voltage is above the reference level, or low if it is below the reference potential. If the inputs of IC1 are swapped over, the output will go high when the input is taken below the reference potential, and low when it is taken above the reference voltage.

Latch-Up

It is worth mentioning here that there are operational amplifier style devices which are specifically designed for use in voltage comparator applications. These often have open collector outputs, and require a load resistor connected between the output and the positive supply rail. True voltage comparators can normally operate with their inputs at any voltages within the limits of the supply voltages. This is not true of most operational amplifiers, which will not function properly with their inputs at potentials close to one of the supply rails, or in some cases with their inputs at voltages close to either supply rail.

Some operational amplifiers suffer from a problem called "latch-up". This is where certain combinations of input voltages result in the output going to the wrong state. With true latch-up, once this has occurred, the output latches in that state. Changes in the input potentials then have no effect on the output. This fault condition is not usually permanent, and switching off the supply for a few seconds and then switching on again will usually restore normal operation. Fortunately, modern operational amplifiers are virtually all guaranteed to be free from latch-up, but are not necessarily guaranteed to operate properly with the inputs at any voltages within the supply limits. If an application may require the voltage comparator to operate with input voltages close to one or other of the supply rails, it might be better to opt for a proper voltage comparator device rather than hoping that an operational amplifier will be able to cope.

Switching Speeds

Operational amplifiers work well in most voltage comparator applications, but it should be borne in mind that no normal operational amplifiers are high speed switching devices. Their outputs switch from one state to the other at far slower rates than most logic integrated circuits. Although a quick examination of the data sheets for a few operational amplifiers might suggest that they could provide output frequencies of a few megahertz with a peak to peak output level virtually equal to the supply potentials, this is not usually the case.

There are two parameters in operational amplifier data sheets which give an indication of how well (or otherwise) fast switching can be accommodated. One of these is the full power bandwidth. This is the highest frequency at which the device can provide its full output voltage swing. Many operational amplifier data sheets include a graph which shows the maximum possible output voltage swing versus output frequency. The 741C for example, can achieve a peak to peak output level of 28 volts at frequencies of up to 10kHz. Above 10kHz the maximum possible output voltage swing falls away very rapidly, and is a mere 3 volts peak to peak at 100kHz. At 500kHz the maximum peak to peak output voltage is only a small fraction of a volt. Although the 741C has unity voltage gain at 1MHz, it is not usable at 1MHz, or at frequencies anywhere near this figure.

22

The other parameter to look for is the slew rate. This is given as so many volts per microsecond, and it is the maximum rate at which the output voltage can change. For the 741C the slew rate is just 0.5 volts per microsecond. At one time various "improved" 741Cs offering higher slew rates were produced, but these now seem to be obsolete. Most modern operational amplifiers offer much higher slew rates, with figures around 10 to 30 times higher than the standard 741C being quite normal. Even these devices are not very fast by normal electronic standards, and the slew rate is something that needs to be kept in mind when using operational amplifiers in any application that requires large output signals switching at high speeds. Where very high switching speeds are essential there are some special operational amplifiers that might be suitable, or a circuit based on discrete transistors might be a more practical proposition.

Trigger Circuits
As pointed out previously, when used as a voltage comparator an operational amplifier can produce intermediate output voltages. In practical applications this will not always be of any practical importance, but in practice it is unlikely that the output would hover at an intermediate voltage anyway. It is far more likely that noise picked up in the wiring, or the noise generated by the operational amplifier itself, will result in output "jitter". This is where the output tends to switch rapidly between the two levels until it eventually stabilises at the new level. Output "jitter" is not usually acceptable, and steps to avoid it are often required.

The normal way of combatting "jitter" is to use positive d.c. feedback, as in the trigger circuit of Figure 1.14. The inverting input is shown as being biased to the 0 volt supply rail via R2, but it can be taken to a reference voltage instead. The input voltage is applied to the non-inverting input via R1. The positive d.c. feedback is applied by R3. Suppose that the input voltage is below the 0 volt reference level, and that the output of IC1 is therefore low. If the input voltage is slowly increased, it will eventually reach the 0 volt reference level, and the output will start to go positive. R3 reduces the voltage at the non-inverting input due to a potential divider

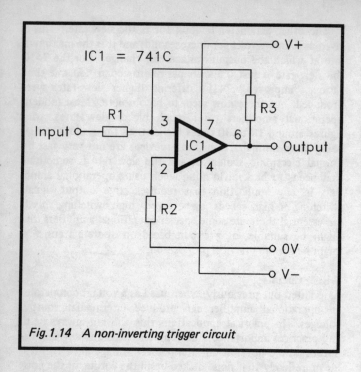

Fig.1.14 A non-inverting trigger circuit

action across R1 and R3. As the output swings more positive, the reduction in the potential at the non-inverting input becomes less. This sends the output more positive, which in turn increases the voltage at the non-inverting input. This gives a regenerative action that results in the output rapidly switching fully positive.

In addition to giving a clean switching action from one output state to the other the positive feedback also introduces hysteresis. This is simply a reluctance to change back to the old state once the output has switched to a new state. With the output now in the high state, the potential divider action across R1 and R3 results in the voltage at the non-inverting input being raised above the input voltage. Previously the output was in the low state, and the potential divider action pulled the non-inverting input to a lower potential than the input level. This means that it was necessary to take the input above the 0 volt reference level in order to trigger the output to the high state. It is then necessary to take the input below the 0 volt reference level in order to trigger the output back to the low state. In other words, there are two switching levels, and not just one.

To give good immunity to "jitter" R3 should be made quite low in value, although it should always be higher in value than R1 in order to prevent the output of the circuit from simply latching. In practice it is often essential to use no more hysteresis than is really necessary, which means making R3 many times higher in value than R1. The reason for this is that using a lot of hysteresis results in two threshold levels that are spaced well apart. In a practical application this will often result in poor accuracy.

For example, a popular application for a trigger circuit is in an electronic thermostat. The input of the trigger circuit would be fed from a temperature sensor, and the output would control a heating element. We will assume here that the temperature sensor is a negative temperature coefficient type. Once a suitable temperature had been reached, the input to the trigger would go below the lower threshold level, and the output would go low. This would switch off the heating element. The voltage from the temperature sensor would then rise as it sensed a decreasing temperature. Eventually the input voltage would go above the upper threshold level, the output of the trigger would go high, and the heating element would be switched back on again. The temperature would then rise, the output voltage from the sensor would decrease, and eventually the heating element would be switched off once more.

This process would continue indefinitely, with the temperature fluctuating between two levels, rather than being maintained at one level. Using simple on/off control of the heating element there is actually no alternative to this method of keeping the temperature between two levels. The amount of hysteresis has to be a good compromise between accuracy on the one hand (little hysteresis), and stability on the other (lots of hysteresis). This usually means adopting the trial and error approach until the best compromise is found.

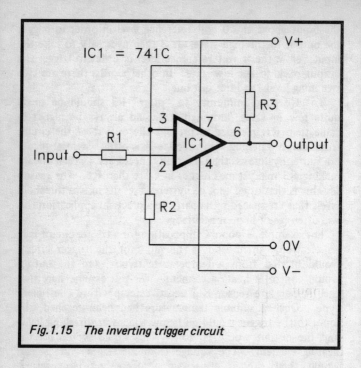

Fig.1.15 *The inverting trigger circuit*

The circuit of Figure 1.14 is for a non-inverting trigger circuit. An inverting trigger circuit is shown in Figure 1.15, and this is just a slight rearrangement of the non-inverting circuit. The hysteresis is provided by R2 and R3, which are the equivalents of R1 and R3 in Figure 1.14.

A.C. Coupling

Operational amplifiers are frequently used in a.c. amplifiers, and are probably used more in this way than in their intended role as d.c. amplifiers. It is possible to have a.c. coupled operational amplifier circuits which operate from dual balanced supplies, but the more usual approach is to use a single supply plus bias resistors. Figure 1.16 shows the circuit for an a.c. coupled non-inverting mode circuit.

R1 and R2 bias the non-inverting input to about half the supply potential. This gives the highest possible peak to peak

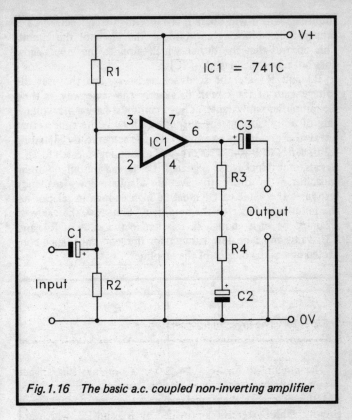

Fig.1.16 The basic a.c. coupled non-inverting amplifier

output level before the onset of clipping. The input impedance of the amplifier is equal to the parallel resistance of R1
and R2. As these two resistors will normally have the same
value, this means that the input impedance is half the value
given to these two components. Looking at things another
way, the value given to these resistors is double the required
input impedance (e.g. use 100k resistors for an input impedance of 50k). In practice there will be a certain amount of
input capacitance which will reduce the input impedance
quite significantly at high frequencies. Of course, this is not
unique to operational amplifier based circuits, and is something that has to be borne in mind when designing any

amplifiers which will operate at fairly high frequencies. C1 is simply a d.c. blocking capacitor at the input of the circuit. This ensures that the device which supplies the input signal does not upset the biasing of IC1.

R3 and R4 are the feedback resistors, and they set the voltage gain of the circuit in exactly the same way as their d.c. amplifier equivalents. The circuit must have a d.c. voltage gain of unity, so that the output bias level is the same as that set at the non-inverting input. This is achieved by including C2 in series with R4. This provides a coupling to earth for a.c. signals, but blocks d.c. signals. C3 is the output coupling capacitor. In order to give an adequate low frequency response, the value of C1 must be high enough in relation to the input impedance of the amplifier. Similarly, the value of C2 must be high enough in relation to the value of R4, and C3's value must be low enough for the load impedance connected across the output of the amplifier.

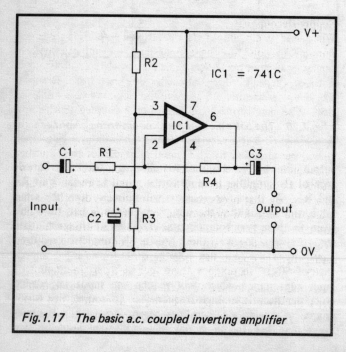

Fig. 1.17   The basic a.c. coupled inverting amplifier

The basic a.c. coupled inverting mode circuit appears in Figure 1.17. R2 and R3 bias the non-inverting input to half the supply potential, and the exact value used for these two resistors is not too important. Very low values are undesirable as they would produce a large current flow through the bias circuit. Very high values might give poor accuracy and problems with pick-up of stray noise. A value of around 4k7 to 100k is usually satisfactory. C2 is not strictly necessary, but with high gain amplifiers there is a risk of instability due to stray feedback to the non-inverting input. C2 decouples any stray feedback and should ensure good stability.

R1 and R4 are the negative feedback network, and they set the voltage gain and input impedance in exactly the same way as the feedback resistors of a d.c. amplifier. C1 and C3 are the input and output coupling capacitors. As for the non-inverting circuit, their values must be high enough to give an adequate low frequency response.

Supply Decoupling

When used as d.c. amplifiers, operational amplifiers are largely immune to noise on the supply lines. I suppose that the operational amplifiers themselves are also largely oblivious to noise on the supply lines when they are used in single supply a.c. coupled circuits, but the amplifier circuits as a whole are not. The main problem is noise being coupled to the non-inverting input via the bias resistor network. Although the noise might be at a very low level at the non-inverting input, it will be amplified by the closed loop gain of the amplifier, and could well be a hundred times stronger at the output. Supply noise finding its way to the output of an a.c. amplifier is a problem that needs to be taken seriously, especially when using the ultra low noise operational amplifiers that are now available. When using these it is very easy to produce circuits where most of the output noise is produced by something other than the operational amplifiers.

This noise coupling is not necessarily a problem with inverting mode circuits, since these usually have a decoupling capacitor from the non-inverting input to earth (C2 of Figure 1.17). It is just a matter of making sure that this capacitor is large enough to decouple any "hum" or other noise which is

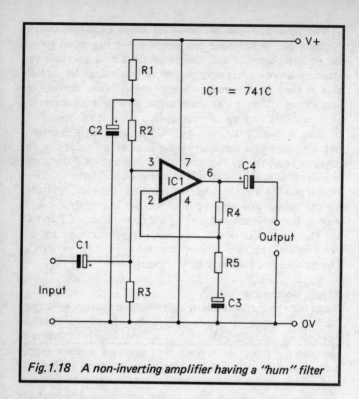

Fig.1.18 A non-inverting amplifier having a "hum" filter

present on the supply rails. Non-inverting amplifiers have the input signal applied to the non-inverting input, so the same approach with these is not a practical proposition!

One way around the problem is to fit a "hum" filter in the bias circuit, as in the circuit of Figure 1.18. The filtering is provided by R1 and C2 which form a simple lowpass filter. R1 must have a much lower value than R2 so that the "hum" filter does not seriously upset the accuracy of the biasing circuit. Alternatively, the value of R2 can be made lower so that the series resistance of R1 and R2 is roughly equal to the value of R3. Figure 1.19 shows an alternative approach to the problem. Here R1 and R2 provide a bias voltage equal to about half the supply potential, and C2 provides the "hum" filtering. R3 biases the non-inverting input to the bias voltage.

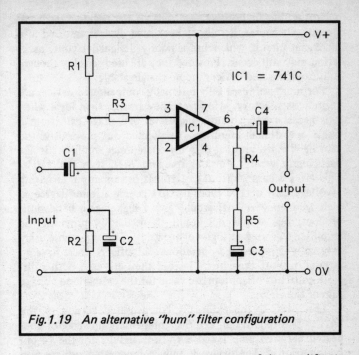

Fig.1.19 An alternative "hum" filter configuration

With this arrangement the input impedance of the amplifier is equal to the value of R3.

Compensation

Most operational amplifiers, including the standard 741C, are fully internally compensated. This simply means that they have an internal capacitor which provides high frequency roll-off. Although this capacitor might seem to be unnecessary, there are practical difficulties if the response is not rolled-off at high frequencies. The main problem is that stray capacitances can result in large phase shifts through the negative feedback circuit at high frequencies. These phase shifts can be large enough to produce oscillation at high frequencies. Surprisingly perhaps, the lower the closed loop voltage gain of the amplifier, the greater the risk of oscillation occurring.

A fully internally compensated operational amplifier can be used at voltage gains of unity or above without oscillation occurring due to positive feedback via the negative feedback circuit. Of course, if fully compensated devices are used in a high gain circuit which has a poorly designed layout, oscillation may still occur. Provided they are used sensibly though, fully compensated devices should remain stable.

For most purposes fully internally compensated devices are entirely satisfactory. However, they are less than ideal when it is necessary to obtain a high level of voltage gain from a single operational amplifier. As pointed out previously, the gain bandwidth product of most operational amplifiers is not particularly great. For the standard 741C it is just 1MHz. This gives a bandwidth of just 10kHz for an amplifier having a voltage gain of 100 times (40dB). Using a lesser degree of high frequency roll-off would give a higher gain bandwidth product, but would not result in oscillation provided the amplifier was used at high voltage gains. This is possible using externally compensated operational amplifiers. These have no internal roll-off capacitor. Instead they are used with a discrete capacitor of appropriate value for the closed loop voltage gain of the circuit.

The 748C is the externally compensated version of the 741C. This requires an external compensation capacitor connected between pins 1 and 8 (pins 3 and 12 for the 14 pin d.i.l. version). The device is fully compensated using a 30p capacitor, and in normal use it would obviously be used with a lower value capacitor in order to obtain increased bandwidth. Figure 1.20 shows the open loop voltage gain of the 748C when it is used with a 30p compensation capacitor at unity voltage gain, and a 2p compensation at a gain of 100 times. It will be seen from this that a roughly tenfold increase in bandwidth is obtained using the 2p compensation capacitor. This permits an amplifier having a closed loop gain of 100 times to achieve a bandwidth of 100kHz, which is rather more useful than the 10kHz bandwidth obtained from an equivalent amplifier based on the 741C.

A useful side-effect of using external compensation is that it also gives improved power bandwidth and slew rate ratings. The 741C has a slew rate of only 0.5V per microsecond, but at a voltage gain of 10 times (20dB) the 748C can achieve a slew rate of 5.5 volts per microsecond.

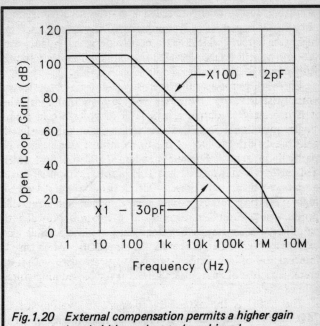

Fig.1.20 External compensation permits a higher gain bandwidth product to be achieved

Some operational amplifiers have partial internal compensation. The NE5534 for instance, is internally compensated for closed loop voltage gains of 10 times or greater. It can be used at lower voltage gains, but an external compensation capacitor is then required. When used without external compensation this device has a very useful gain bandwidth product of 10MHz, and a slew rate of some 13 volts per microsecond. The full power bandwidth is 200kHz, which is some 20 times higher than the 741C's full power bandwidth rating.

Although most modern operational amplifiers have full internal compensation, they mostly have much better high frequency performance than the 741C. The popular Bifet operational amplifiers (LF351N, TL071C, etc.) have gain bandwidth products of about 4MHz, and an open loop frequency response similar to that shown in Figure 1.21.

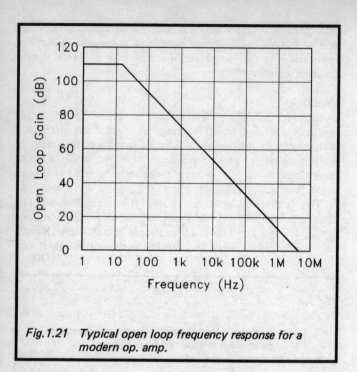

Fig.1.21 Typical open loop frequency response for a modern op. amp.

At an open loop voltage gain of 100 times this permits a bandwidth of around 40kHz to be obtained. This is not a vast improvement on the 741C, but it makes the difference between a bandwidth of about half the audio range for the 741C, and double the audio range for the bifet devices. The slew rates and power bandwidths of the bifet devices are vastly better than those of the 741C. They are typically about 13 volts per microsecond and 100kHz respectively.

Where audio amplifiers having voltage gains of several hundred times or more are required, it is not possible to obtain the required gain using a single operational amplifier. Even using modern operational amplifiers or externally compensated types, it is unlikely that the required gain could be obtained over the full audio bandwidth. In cases where it is just about possible to achieve the required voltage gain and bandwidth, it would almost certainly be better to use a two stage amplifier with each operational amplifier working well within its capabilities. Except in genuinely non-critical applications, a two stage amplifier will provide better distortion performance.

Feedback

Operational amplifiers do not have to be used with simple feedback provided purely by resistors. They are often used with diodes to provide some form of non-linear feedback, or with capacitors to provide frequency selective feedback. The most simple form of non-linear feedback is to use two diodes in the feedback circuit, as in Figure 1.22.

This is the standard clipping amplifier configuration. The circuit is basically just a standard non-inverting type, but diodes D1 and D2 have been connected in parallel with feedback resistor R4. With low output levels (up to about one

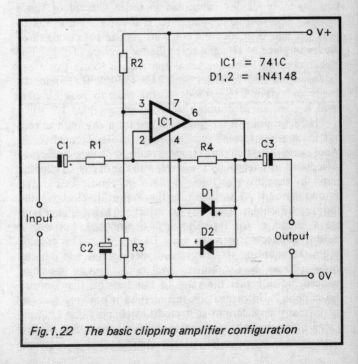

Fig.1.22 The basic clipping amplifier configuration

volt peak to peak) neither D1 nor D2 are brought to the threshold of conduction. The amplifier operates as a standard inverting type having a closed loop voltage gain dictated only by R1 and R4. At output levels of more than about one volt peak to peak the diodes start to conduct. D1 conducts on negative half cycles — D2 conducts on positive half cycles. On signal peaks D1 and D2 therefore shunt R4, and reduce the closed loop voltage gain of the circuit.

Silicon diodes have well defined forward threshold voltages. Below this voltage the forward resistance is many megohms. Above the threshold potential the forward resistance drops very rapidly as the applied voltage is increased. In the current context this results in heavy clipping of the output signal, with the output level never going much higher than about 1.2 volts peak to peak no matter how high the input level is made. Higher clipping levels can be obtained by using two or more diodes connected in series, instead of single diodes. The output clipping level is about 1.2 volts peak to peak per pair of diodes (e.g. 3.6 volts peak to peak using three diodes in place of D1, and three diodes in place of D2). For higher clipping levels the usual approach is to use two zener diodes connected in series, and back-to-back (i.e. anode to anode or cathode to cathode). The peak to peak clipping level is then about double the zener voltage, plus 1.2 volts.

"Hard" clipping is the form required for many applications, but for some purposes "soft" clipping is more appropriate. In other words, it is sometimes preferable to have the clipping introduced at a relatively low level, with the degree of clipping gradually increasing as the input level is raised. This gives a limited amount of variation in the output level above the clipping threshold. One way of achieving soft clipping is to use a circuit of the type shown in Figure 1.21, but with a resistor connected in series with D1 and D2. This resistor limits the shunting effect of the diodes on R4, and permits some increase in the output level once clipping has commenced. The higher the value of this resistor, the "softer" the clipping. Unfortunately, this method is not very successful in many applications as it produces clipping that is introduced quite abruptly at a certain threshold level. It is often a very gradual introduction of the clipping that is required.

Probably the only simple way of achieving this type of clipping is to use germanium diodes for D1 and D2. These start to introduce the clipping at quite a low level, and give a very subtle form of clipping. The maximum output level is much lower using germanium diodes, and is unlikely to exceed 500 millivolts peak to peak. A few applications require very carefully controlled non-linear feedback which distorts the output signal in a particular way. For example, function generators produce the sinewave output signal by distorting the output from a triangular waveform generator. In order to do this well it is essential to distort the input signal in just the right way, and this requires complex diode and resistor networks.

Practical applications for clipping amplifiers often require the output to switch at quite a high frequency. The 0.5 volts per microsecond slew rate and 10kHz full power bandwidth of the 741C make it unsuitable for many applications of this type. More modern devices having slew rates of 10 volts per microsecond or more plus a full power bandwidth of 100kHz or greater are better suited to clipping applications that involve fast switching output signals. It should also be borne in mind that clipping amplifiers often have high voltage gains so that the signal is boosted sufficiently to give strong clipping. This can result in quite a high noise level at the output. While this is unlikely to be a problem when a heavily clipping output signal is present, it can cause problems in applications where the input signal is of an intermittent nature. It can often be advantageous to base a clipping amplifier on a very low noise operational amplifier.

Active Rectifiers

A silicon or germanium diode can be used to rectify an a.c. input signal, but both types of component are far from ideal if good linearity is required. An ideal rectifier would have a forward resistance that remained constant at all input voltages. The output signal would then be exactly the same as the input signal, but with one set of half cycles removed or inverted. The resistance of semiconductor diodes varies considerably with changes in the applied voltage. In the case of silicon diodes there is the problem that they fail to conduct significantly until the applied voltage reaches about 0.5 volts or so. This gives a problem that goes beyond a simple lack of linearity. The linearity is so poor that the bottom part of the waveform is totally absent on the output waveform.

Operational amplifiers can be used to provide precision rectification from normal silicon or germanium diodes. The basic idea is to use a diode or diodes in the feedback circuit so as to give a distorted output signal. The distortion on the output signal is the opposite of that produced by the diode. Therefore, feeding the distorted signal through the diode gives a rectified but otherwise undistorted output signal. Figure 1.23 shows the basic circuit for a precision half wave rectifier. Since the output never goes negative, the single supply version of Figure 1.24 will work just as well provided a suitable operational amplifier is used.

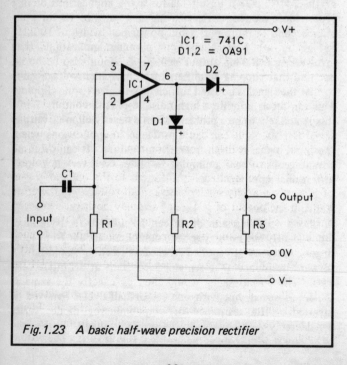

Fig.1.23 A basic half-wave precision rectifier

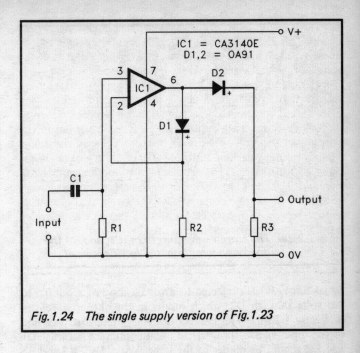

Fig.1.24   The single supply version of Fig.1.23

The circuit is basically a non-inverting amplifier, but diode D1 is used in place of the normal feedback resistor. D1 does not conduct significantly at low output voltages, giving a high feedback resistance, and an extremely high closed loop voltage gain. In fact the closed loop voltage gain will not be significantly different to the open loop gain of IC1. Even a very small positive input voltage will therefore result in the output of IC1 going strongly positive. However, once the output has gone sufficiently positive, D1 starts to conduct strongly, and the closed loop gain falls to a much lower level. In fact the voltage gain drops back to little more than unity once the forward threshold voltage of D1 has been exceeded.

If a silicon diode is used for D1, a sinewave input signal gives an output signal from IC1 similar to that of Figure 1.25(a). This is rectified and quite heavily distorted, with all the voltages being raised by about 0.5 to 0.6 volts. The output

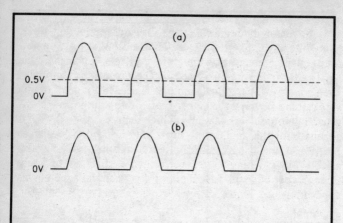

Fig.1.25(a) The output waveform from IC1, and (b) the
output waveform from the rectifier circuit

signal across R3 is subjected to a voltage drop of about 0.5 to
0.6 volts through D2, which results in the output waveform
of Figure 1.25(b). This is a rectified and non-distorted version
of the input signal. In order to obtain optimum linearity, D1
and D2 should be diodes of the same type. Also, R2 and R3
should have the same value.

Although precision rectifiers based on silicon diodes can
work quite well, this is one application where germanium
diodes have a definite advantage. This type of circuit is more
demanding on the operational amplifier than it might at first
appear. It relies on a large amount of feedback to provide an
accurately distorted output from the operational amplifier.
This in turn relies on there being a large difference between
the open and closed loop gains of the operational amplifier.
At low frequencies any operational amplifier should provide
accurate results. At high frequencies the open loop gains of
many operational amplifiers become too low to give good
results. Even at the higher audio frequencies results may be
rather poor using a 741C or similar. Another point to bear in
mind is that the output of the operational amplifier has to
switch very rapidly at the beginning and end of each half
cycle. At high operating frequencies the slew rate of the

operational amplifier becomes an important factor.

Germanium diodes have lower forward conduction threshold voltages, and better linearity than silicon types. Counteracting their non-linearity therefore puts less demand on the bandwidth and switching speed of the operational amplifier. Even so, a fast operational amplifier is needed for good results at anything beyond the upper limit of the audio range. A general purpose germanium diode such as the OA91 is adequate for this application, but a gold bonded type such as the OA85 might give slightly better results. A Schottky silicon diode offers better performance than an ordinary silicon type, but still falls short of a germanium type in this application.

Equalisation

Many applications require an audio amplifier which has a tailored frequency response. For example, tape head and magnetic cartridge preamplifiers must both provide this equalisation in order to obtain a flat frequency response from the overall system. A simple 6dB per octave roll off can be obtained by adding a capacitor in parallel with the feedback resistor. This is the purpose of C2 in the circuit of Figure 1.26. At low frequencies the impedance of C2 will be high in relation to the value of R3, and it will not have a significant affect on the circuit. At higher frequencies the impedance of C2 is lower, and at a certain frequency it will be the same as the resistance/impedance of R3. At this frequency C2 effectively shunts R3 to half its normal value, and the closed loop gain of the amplifier is reduced by 50% (reduced by 6dB). Above this frequency each doubling of the input frequency results in a halving of C2's impedance, giving a roll-off that ultimately reaches about 6dB per octave.

Equalisation can also be applied to an inverting mode amplifier, as in the circuit of Figure 1.27. There is an important difference between the two modes in that the non-inverting circuit can never have a voltage gain of less than unity. A large amount of high frequency roll-off is therefore only possible if the amplifier has a high closed loop voltage gain at low frequencies. If the amplifier has a closed loop gain of (say) 12dB, then the maximum high frequency roll-off

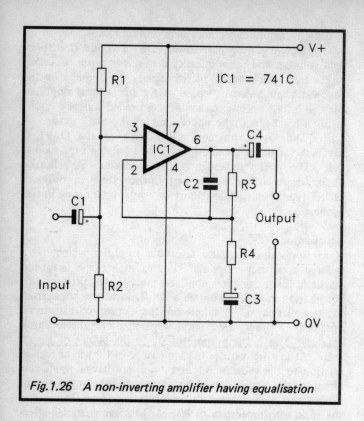

Fig.1.26 A non-inverting amplifier having equalisation

that can be achieved is also 12dB.

The inverting mode circuit can have a closed loop voltage gain of less than unity, and it can therefore provide unlimited high frequency attenuation. There is a potential difficulty in that gains of less than unity might result in instability. In practice this is not usually a problem. However, if necessary the problem can be overcome by using a resistor (R4) in series with the roll-off capacitor to limit the minimum closed loop gain to a safe level. In some applications this resistor would be included anyway, in order to remove the roll-off above a certain frequency. In fact equalisation sometimes requires a feedback network consisting of several resistors and capacitors

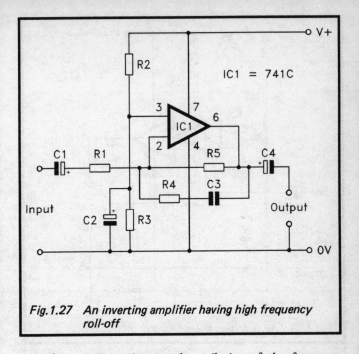

Fig.1.27 *An inverting amplifier having high frequency roll-off*

in order to give quite complex tailoring of the frequency response.

Bear in mind that adding a capacitor direct across the feedback resistor results in the closed loop gain falling to unity at high frequencies. An operational amplifier used in this way must be a fully compensated type, or it will almost certainly oscillate at a high frequency.

A.C. Triggering

The subject of d.c. trigger circuits was discussed earlier, but triggers are also used a great deal in a.c. signal processing circuits. Their main use is in applications where a relatively slow output signal is used to drive a device that requires a rapidly switching input signal. No matter how slowly the input voltage varies, the output of a trigger circuit will always switch rapidly from one state to the other as an input threshold level is crossed. The hysteresis can counteract noise on

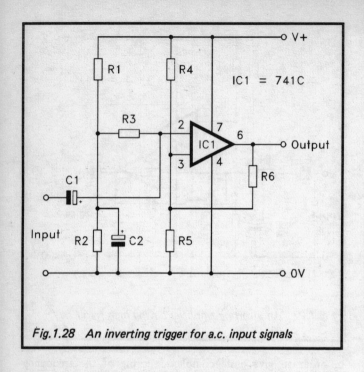

Fig. 1.28 An inverting trigger for a.c. input signals

an a.c. input signal, in exactly the same way as it combats noise on a very slow input signal from a sensor.

An a.c. trigger is basically just a d.c. type plus some biasing components. Figure 1.28 shows the circuit diagram for an inverting trigger circuit. R4 and R5 bias the non-inverting input, and R6 provides the positive feedback. The degree of hysteresis is therefore dependent on the value of R6 relative to the value of R4 and R5. R1, R2, and C2 provide a bias voltage which is coupled to the non-inverting input of IC1 via R3. C1 provides input coupling. Figure 1.29 shows the circuit diagram for a non-inverting a.c. trigger circuit, which is just a slightly rearranged version of the inverting circuit.

Trigger circuits are often used in applications which require fairly high output frequencies, and fast switching times. This means that something more than a 741C will often be required. Remember that the 741C has a full power bandwidth

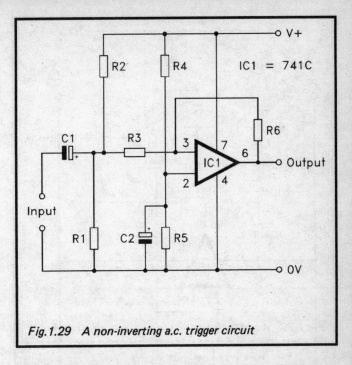

Fig.1.29 A non-inverting a.c. trigger circuit

of only 10kHz. Even at frequencies of a few kilohertz its output might switch too slowly. Modern operational amplifiers having full power bandwidths of about 100kHz to 200kHz are more appropriate to applications which involve high output frequencies.

A.C. Differential

Differential amplifiers for use with a.c. signals are useful in processing circuits where anti-phase mixing is required. A number of a.c. processing circuits operate by mixing a processed signal and an unprocessed signal so that one partially cancels out the other. This can be achieved by using a summing mode mixer circuit with an inverter added ahead of one input, but the differentiate configuration shown in Figure 1.30 is a more simple alternative. This is much the same as the d.c. configuration, but with added biasing components,

45

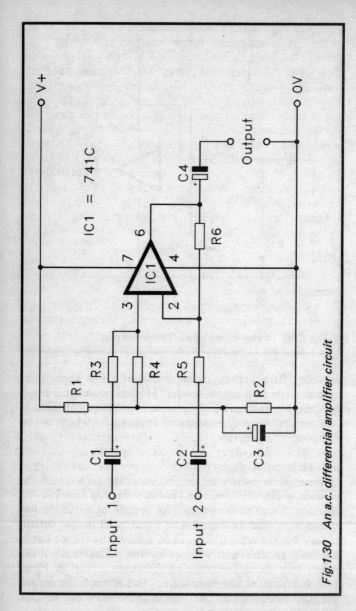

Fig. 1.30 An a.c. differential amplifier circuit

plus input and output coupling capacitors.

This is one application where the humble 741C will often prove to be perfectly satisfactory. The only exceptions are where high frequencies are involved, or very low noise and distortion levels are required. Higher performance operational amplifiers are then required. It is worth making the point that it tends to be difficult to obtain precise cancelling over a wide frequency range. This is due to stray capacitance causing phase shifts at higher frequencies. These frequency dependent phase shifts are not a unique property of operational amplifier circuits, and are something that occurs with any a.c. amplifier. Using low resistance values helps to minimise unwanted phase shifts. In theory at any rate, an operational amplifier having a low input capacitance should be better than one having a high input capacitance (i.e. a bipolar type should be better than any form of f.e.t. input device).

Output Impedance

The output impedance figures for operational amplifiers tend to cause a certain amount of confusion. The output impedance of the 741C at low frequencies is 75 ohms, and when used with a lot of feedback it becomes much less. With 100% negative feedback the output impedance is in the region of one ohm. This tends to give the impression that large output currents can be supplied by an operational amplifier. A theoretical operational amplifier has an output impedance of zero and can supply any required output current, but actual operational amplifiers fall well short of theoretical perfection.

Although the output impedances of operational amplifiers are quite low, they can usually supply maximum output currents of no more than a few milliamps. The 741C for instance, will typically supply just 25 milliamps with the output short circuited to one of the supply rails. In normal operation it would be used with a maximum output current of very much less than this. The output impedance is low in that loading the output by a few milliamps results in an insignificant change in the output voltage. However, if an output current of more than a few milliamps is drawn, the overload protection circuits come into operation and the

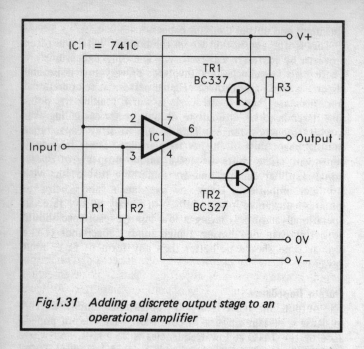

*Fig.1.31   Adding a discrete output stage to an
operational amplifier*

output voltage changes drastically. This is not a major draw-back because operational amplifiers are mainly used in low level applications. On the other hand, there are numerous applications where a high power operational amplifier could be put to good use.

One way of obtaining higher output currents is to add a discrete class B output stage, as shown in Figure 1.31. This is a non-inverting amplifier, but the add-on output stage will work just as well with any normal operational amplifier configuration. Note that the negative feedback is taken from output of the circuit as a whole, and not from the output of IC1. The negative feedback therefore counteracts any distortion added by the output stage. In practice this distortion will be quite high due to the cross-over distortion of the output stage. At low frequencies the negative feedback is so great that there will be no significant cross-over distortion. At higher frequencies the open loop gain of IC1 is much lower, as is the amount of negative feedback applied to the circuit. The cross-over distortion then becomes quite high.

Using an operational amplifier having a high gain bandwidth product helps to keep down the high frequency distortion, but will not give hi-fi performance. It is better to add a bias circuit at the bases of TR1 and TR2 to reduce the innate cross-over distortion of the circuit, than to rely on masses of feedback to cure the problem. Using a pair of complementary output transistors permits output currents of up to about 200 milliamps to be achieved. Higher output currents can be obtained using Darlington power devices, or some other high gain configuration.

These days there are power operational amplifiers which offer a real alternative to an ordinary operational amplifier plus a discrete output stage. Using a power operational amplifier it is possible to obtain output currents of up to a few amps, and there are no problems with discrete bias circuits to avoid excessive cross-over distortion. This is all taken care of by the internal circuits of the operational amplifier. Although at one time power operational amplifiers were very expensive, many of these devices are now very competitive with the discrete alternatives. They are certainly worth considering for any d.c. or low frequency application that requires output currents of up to a few amps.

Oscillators

Operational amplifiers can be used in numerous oscillator configurations, but there are two or three popular configurations which satisfy most requirements. If a very simple oscillator having a (roughly) squarewave output signal is required, the relaxation oscillator circuit of Figure 1.32 is the usual choice. IC1 operates as a very simple inverting trigger circuit having positive feedback provided by R3. C1 and R4 are a C − R timing circuit. The output of IC1 goes high initially, and C1 therefore charges via R4. This continues until the charge voltage on C1 exceeds the upper trigger threshold voltage. The output of IC1 then triggers to the low state, and C1 starts to discharge via R4. This continues until the charge potential on C1 falls to the lower trigger threshold voltage, and the output of IC1 then switches back to the high state. C1 then starts

49

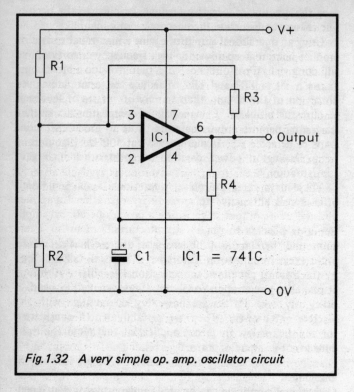

Fig. 1.32 A very simple op. amp. oscillator circuit

to charge via R4 again, and the circuit oscillates indefinitely with C1 being repeatedly charged and discharged.

The operating frequency is obviously governed to a large extent by the values of C1 and R4. Since C1 can be an electrolytic type, and the circuit will operate properly with R4 at high values, very low output frequencies can be obtained. The degree of hysteresis also has a large effect on the output frequency. A small amount of hysteresis means that the charge on C1 only has to rise and fall by small amounts during each cycle. This gives a high output frequency for a given set of timing component values. Using a large amount of hysteresis produces large voltage changes across C1, and relatively long charge/discharge times. This gives a relatively low output frequency.

Although the theoretical output waveform is a perfect squarewave, in practice the mark-space ratio is unlikely to be exactly 1 : 1. This is due to the non-symmetrical nature of most operational amplifier output stages. However, by adjusting the ratio of R1 to R2 it should be possible to produce a 1 : 1 mark-space ratio. This is a matter of making the non-symmetry of R1 and R2 match that of the operational amplifier. Once again, the speed of the operational amplifier is often an important consideration. It is no good expecting a 741C to produce a perfect squarewave at 50kHz. High output frequencies require fast operational amplifiers. Incidentally, a sort of non-linear triangular waveform is available at pin 2 of IC1, but this is at a fairly high impedance and should only be used via a buffer stage.

Function Generator

The circuit of Figure 1.33 is one of the most widely used operational amplifier configurations, and it is for a basic function generator. It provides square and triangular waveforms. It is similar in operation to the relaxation oscillator described previously, with C2 being repeatedly charged and discharged via R4. IC1b operates as the trigger circuit. However, with this configuration an integrator (based on IC1a) has been added at the input of the trigger circuit. This results in C2 charging and discharging at a linear rate, giving a low impedance linear triangular waveform at the output of IC1a. The trigger circuit provides a (roughly) squarewave output signal, as before.

A fast operational amplifier is needed for high output frequencies, even if it is only the triangular output signal that is required. The important factor here is that the triangular waveform is dependent on the quality of the squarewave signal, since the triangular signal is effectively derived from the squarewave type. Any irregularities in the squarewave signal affect the charge and discharge rates of C2, and reduce the linearity of the triangular output signal. Apart from a lack of switching speed, there is also overshoot to consider. This is where a spike is produced on the squarewave signal immediately after each output transition. This leads to glitches on the triangular waveform. For operation at frequencies of more

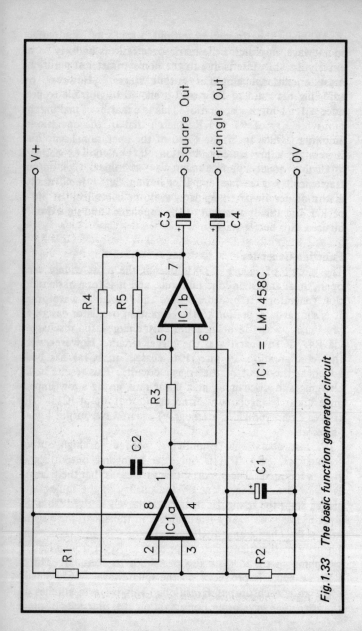

Fig.1.33   The basic function generator circuit

than a few kilohertz it is necessary to use a fast and stable operational amplifier. Best results are generally produced using a fast, fully internally compensated operational amplifier. An externally compensated type will probably give faster rise and fall times at the squarewave output, but may also give severe overshoot.

Sinewave Oscillator

Generating a low quality sinewave signal is quite easy, but producing a really low distortion sinewave signal is a different matter. It requires an amplifier having very low noise and distortion levels, plus very accurately regulated positive feedback. The usual approach to the problem, and one which is difficult to better, is to use a Wien oscillator plus a self-heating thermistor to control the level of feedback. Operational amplifiers are an ideal basis for circuits of this type. Figure

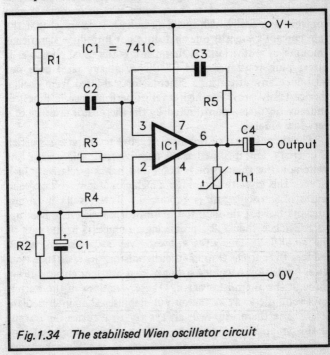

Fig. 1.34   The stabilised Wien oscillator circuit

1.34 shows the circuit diagram for a thermistor stabilised Wien oscillator.

The Wien network consists of two resistors (R3 and R5) and two capacitors (C2 and C3). It is connected so that it provides positive feedback over what is basically just a non-inverting mode amplifier. At a certain frequency there is zero phase shift through the Wien network, and provided the closed loop voltage gain of the amplifier is greater than the losses through the Wien network, the circuit will oscillate at this frequency. A voltage gain of only about 10dB is needed to produce oscillation, but in order to produce a good quality sinewave signal the voltage gain of the circuit must be just right. Fractionally too little gain and oscillation will die away to nothing – slightly too much gain and oscillation becomes so strong that the output waveform becomes clipped.

The only way of ensuring that a good quality output signal is always generated is to have some sort of automatic gain control. For really high quality results it is essential that the gain control system is one that does not introduce significant amounts of distortion. A thermistor is the usual choice as it offers pure resistance, and (in theory at any rate) does not introduce any distortion. Thermistor stabilised Wien oscillators certainly provide a high level of performance in practice, and any distortion contributed by the thermistor must be of a very low order.

The thermistor is of the usual negative temperature coefficient variety, and it is used as the negative feedback resistor. At switch-on the thermistor is cool, and it has a relatively high value. This gives the amplifier a high closed loop voltage gain, and strong oscillation is produced. This results in strong currents flowing through the thermistor, causing it to heat up. Its resistance then falls, producing a reduction in the gain of the amplifier. This gives a lower level output signal, which reduces the current through the thermistor. Its resistance then rises, oscillation becomes stronger, and a higher current flows through the thermistor again. These variations in the output level soon die away as the output stabilises at an intermediate level. The thermistor will always try to regulate the output at this amplitude, and will to a large extent compensate for variations in output loading, changes in the Wien network values, etc.

Even the humble 741C gives good results in this type of circuit at low frequencies. Distortion levels of well under 1% are obtained over all but the upper end of the audio range. However, for very high performance levels a more modern operational amplifier is needed. Any operational amplifier which is intended for use in very low noise and distortion audio preamplifiers should give excellent results in a Wien oscillator. Distortion levels of under 0.1% are possible over the audio range, with a distortion figure of 0.01% or less being achievable at middle and low audio frequencies.

P.W.M.

Pulse width modulation is used in two main circumstances. One is where a d.c. level must be coupled through a system that can only handle a.c. signals. The other is where a d.c. level or audio signal must be coupled through a system that offers very poor linearity. A conventional pulse width modulator consists of a triangular waveform generator and a comparator, as in Figure 1.35. The output of the circuit goes high while the input voltage is at a higher potential than the triangular signal, and low when it is at a lower voltage.

With the input at 0 volts, the circuit produces the waveforms shown in Figure 1.36(b). Here the upper waveform is the output from the oscillator, the dotted line is the input voltage, and the lower waveform is the output signal. As one would expect, with the triangular signal swinging symmetrically about the input level, the output signal is a squarewave having an accurate 1 : 1 mark-space ratio. Raising the input voltage gives the waveforms of Figure 1.36(a). Now the input signal is at the higher voltage for the majority of the time, and the mark-space ratio is quite high. Taking the input voltage strongly negative has the opposite effect. The oscillator signal is positive of the input signal for the majority of the time, give an output signal having a low mark-space ratio (Figure 1.36(c)).

Although a pulse width modulator might seem to be very clever but pointless, it does have practical applications. The important point to note is that the average output voltage changes in sympathy with the input voltage. If the oscillator

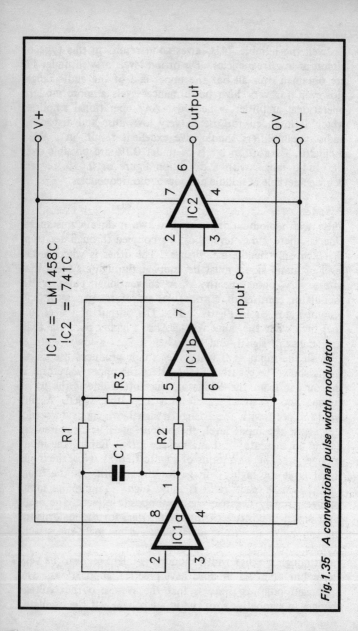

Fig. 1.35 A conventional pulse width modulator

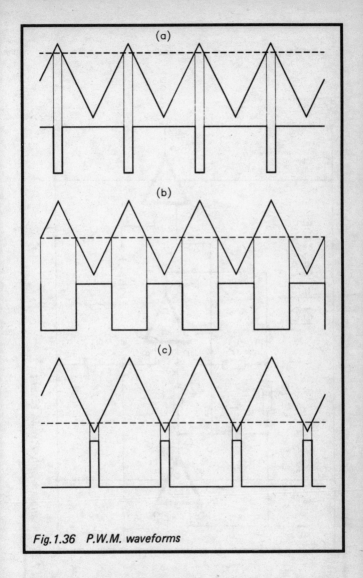

Fig. 1.36   P.W.M. waveforms

signal was to have a peak-to-peak level equal to the supply
voltages, the average output voltage would actually be the same

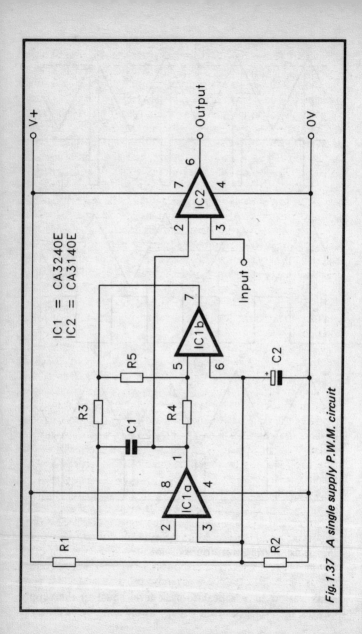

Fig. 1.37 A single supply P.W.M. circuit

IC1 = CA3240E
IC2 = CA3140E

58

as the input voltage. In practice this can not be easily achieved, but there is a linear relationship between the input voltage and the average output voltage. In order to recover the average output voltage from the pulsing output signal it is merely necessary to use some strong lowpass filtering.

Systems of this type are often used to transmit audio signals through a device which does not provide good linearity, such as an opto-isolator. The output from the pulse width modulator is just a stream of pulses, and any lack of linearity in their transmission will not produce a lack of linearity in the final output signal. For a low distortion output signal the switching speed of the comparator and the linearity of the triangular signal are the factors that are important.

Using slow operational amplifiers such as the LM1458C and 741C it is only possible to transmit fairly low frequencies through the system. The oscillator frequency must be at least double the maximum input frequency, and should ideally be three or more times the maximum input frequency. Using slow devices a clock frequency of about 2kHz represents a realistic maximum, which represents a bandwidth of about 1kHz or less.

For most practical applications a single supply pulse width modulator circuit will suffice. Figure 1.37 shows the basic circuit for a pulse width modulator of this type. This is based on fast PMOS operational amplifiers which can handle clock frequencies of up to about 50kHz, which just about accommodates the full audio bandwidth of 20kHz. Bifet and other modern devices offer a comparable level of performance. The linearity of the system is still likely to be something less than true hi-fi, but the level of performance is adequate for many practical purposes.

A certain amount of overshoot in the oscillator circuit is less important than one might expect. It will produce kinks in the triangular signal, but only at the signal peaks. This is not important provided the input signal level is suitably restricted, the peaks of the waveform will not play an active role in the p.w.m. process. Severe overshoot is a different matter though, and is likely to produce a severely distorted triangular waveform.

Chapter 2

PRACTICAL CIRCUITS

In this chapter we will consider some practical circuits which demonstrate the advantages of various modern operational amplifiers. The devices featured are all in some way (or ways) superior to the standard 741C and 748C operational amplifiers. They are used in circuits where their improved performance is a real advantage, and not in circuits where the 741C or 748C would be perfectly adequate.

Audio Basics

Operational amplifiers became popular for use in audio equipment quite early in their history. Circuit designers soon realised the ease with which specific voltage gains and input impedances could be set. Also, they could be set very accurately, and with good repeatability. The same was not true of most discrete audio amplifier designs. Apart from those that used operational amplifier style feedback circuits and techniques, voltage gains often varied substantially from one unit to another due to the wide gain tolerances of the transistors used.

Operational amplifiers are now the standard choice for most audio preamplifier applications, and there are numerous operational amplifier integrated circuits which are designed specifically for audio frequency use. The audio performance figures of the standard 741C and 748C operational amplifiers are actually quite respectable, and they are adequate for many audio applications. However, in the more demanding audio preamplifier applications they have some definite shortcomings. The bandwidth, distortion, and noise figures in particular, could be better.

Although the 741C and 748C are still used in audio preamplifiers, they have to a large extent been ousted by Bifet devices such as the TLO71CP, TLO81CP, and LF351N. These are basically bipolar operational amplifiers, but they have Jfet input stages. The original operational amplifiers which had Jfet input stages were basically just ordinary 741Cs, but with discrete Jfet input transistors within the same encapsulation. The Bifet devices are manufactured using advanced techniques which permit the Jfet input transistors and the bipolar transistors to be incorporated on the same chip.

The gain bandwidth product of fully compensated Bifet operational amplifiers is about three to four megahertz, which is a useful but far from massive improvement on the 741C. It does permit a voltage gain of 100 times (40dB) to be achieved over substantially more than the full audio bandwidth, and this is sufficient for most practical purposes. The full power bandwidth is around 100kHz, which is some ten times better than the 741C. The improvement in slew rate is even greater, at about 26 times higher than the figure for the 741C.

The distortion performance of Bifet operational amplifiers is quite impressive. The LF351N for example, has less than 0.02% total harmonic distortion when used with a voltage gain of 10 times (20dB), a 20 volt peak-to-peak output level, and a load impedance of 10k. This distortion performance is maintained over the full 20kHz audio bandwidth.

One respect in which the Bifet devices are not a great improvement over the 741C is their audio noise performance. When the Bifet operational amplifiers were first introduced, many people tried using them instead of 741Cs in various pieces of audio gear. They were expecting the new "wonder" chips to make a huge improvement in the background noise level of their audio equipment. The improvement obtained was not particularly large in most cases, and some users found that there was no obvious improvement at all.

The Bifet devices do have substantially better noise figures than the 741C, but at the time of their introduction the improvement tended to be exaggerated a little. The typical noise figure for the 741C seems to vary from one manufacturer to another, but it is usually quoted as 45 nanovolts per root hertz. Most Bifet operational amplifiers have noise figures of around 12 to 25 nanovolts per root hertz. An improvement in the signal to noise ratio of 6dB or so would be a realistic expectation, but the improvement of about 20dB or more that some users were anticipating was simply not possible.

When using Bifet devices it should be borne in mind that they are not affected by source impedances in quite the same way as devices having bipolar input transistors. With a bipolar input stage, the lower the source impedance, the lower the noise level. Bifet devices also produce less noise when used with low source impedances, but the variation in noise performance over a range of source impedances is very much less. A Bifet device is therefore unlikely to offer much of an improvement over a 741C in an amplifier which has a low input impedance, and which is being driven from a low impedance source. It would be expected to offer a much more substantial improvement in an amplifier which has a high input impedance, and which is being driven from a high impedance source.

Although many users seem to be under the impression that Bifet types are the lowest noise operational amplifiers, this is definitely not the case. There are now a number of bipolar input operational amplifiers which offer superior performance to Bifet types such as the TLO71C and LF356N. Probably the best known of these are the NE5532 (dual) and NE5534 (single) operational amplifiers. There are also "A" suffix versions of these devices which have slightly superior audio performance. The NE5532 has a noise figure of 5 nanovolts per root hertz, and the noise figure for the NE5534 is 4 nanovolts per root hertz (3.5 nanovolts per root hertz for the "A" version). There are now operational amplifiers having even lower noise levels, and noise figures of around 2 nanovolts per root hertz are typical of these super low noise devices.

Modern low noise operational amplifiers clearly offer vastly superior performance to the 741C, and are a much better option for audio preamplifier applications where high gain and low noise are required. The NE5534A provides an improvement in the signal to noise ratio of well over 20dB when used in place of a 741C. Its gain bandwidth product is much superior at 10MHz, giving a 100kHz bandwidth with a closed loop gain of 100 times (40dB). The distortion performance of the NE5534A, NE5532A, etc., is vastly superior to that of the 741C. The only drawback of high quality audio operational amplifiers is that they are relatively expensive. Many of these components are still quite affordable though, and considering the level of performance they offer should be considered real bargains.

It is worth making the point that operational amplifiers having MOSFET input stages (CA3140E, CA3240E, etc.) are not primarily intended for use in audio circuits. In most respects they have quite respectable audio performance figures, but their noise figures are only marginal improvements on the 741C. For audio applications Bifet devices offer significantly better performance at a comparable price.

R.I.A.A. Preamplifier

Gramophone records now seem to have given way to compact cassettes, compact discs, etc., and few new recordings are made available on vinyl discs. On the other hand, there must be countless gramophone records in existence, and people will presumably still be playing their favourite LPs for many years to come. The output level from a magnetic cartridge is not very large, and is typically just a few millivolts r.m.s. The input stage of a magnetic cartridge preamplifier must therefore be based on a low noise device if it is to give true hi-fi performance.

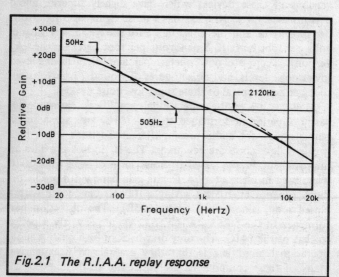

Fig.2.1 The R.I.A.A. replay response

A magnetic cartridge preamplifier must provide equalisation. Bass cut is used during the recording process to prevent excessive groove modulations, and treble boost is used as a form of basic noise reduction. The preamplifier must provide complementary bass boost and treble cut. The R.I.A.A. replay characteristic is shown in Figure 2.1. The dotted line is the response usually shown in text books, but the true response is something more like the solid line.

Figure 2.2 shows the circuit diagram for a practical R.I.A.A. preamplifier. R2 and R3 set the input impedance at 50k, which is suitable for most magnetic pickups. R2 and R3 should have a value of 200k if the preamplifier is to be used with a cartridge that has a recommended load impedance of 100k. The equalisation is easily provided using a C — R network in the feedback path. The twin kinks of the R.I.A.A. playback response require the use of two resistors and two capacitors (R4, R5, C3, and C4). Getting the right response is a bit tricky using preferred values, but quite accurate results can be obtained using values from the E24 series. The ideal time constants are 75 and 3180 microseconds, and R5 needs to be about 12 times the value of R4.

The gain of the circuit is a little over 50 times (34dB) at middle frequencies. This will produce an output of about one volt peak to peak or more from some cartridges, but with low output types the output level could be under 500 millivolts peak to peak. If necessary, the gain can be boosted slightly by making R6 a little lower in value. However, if a large increase in the output level is needed it would be better to add a low gain amplifier stage, rather than boosting the gain of this circuit to the point where it could compromise performance.

The performance of the circuit is very good, and an unweighted signal to noise ratio of better than 80dB should be achieved. Due to the high frequency cut provided by the equalisation, and the relatively small amount of high frequency noise on the output, the weighted noise figure should be substantially better. The distortion level is extremely low over the full audio range.

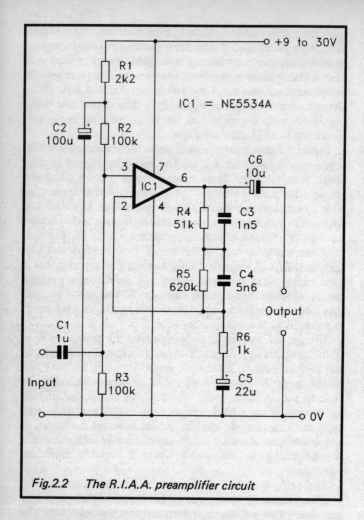

Fig.2.2   The R.I.A.A. preamplifier circuit

Tape Preamplifier

The output level from the low impedance tape head of a cassette deck is extremely small. It is typically only about 200 microvolts r.m.s., which makes it quite difficult to obtain a really good signal to noise ratio. Matters are helped significantly by the fact that equalisation is needed, and this results in substantially reduced high frequency noise. The output from a tape head rises at 6dB per octave, and a certain amount of high frequency boost is used during the recording process as part of a simple form of noise reduction. In theory, a substantial amount of treble cut is needed during playback in order to give a flat overall frequency response. In practice a far lesser degree of treble cut is needed due to imperfections in "real world" tapes and recording/playback heads.

Figure 2.3 shows the circuit diagram for a practical cassette tape preamplifier. IC1 is used as a non-inverting input stage which has equalisation provided by the C − R feedback circuit. The input impedance of the amplifier is 50k, but this is shunted to a more suitable figure of about 4k by R1. It is sometimes undesirable to have a high value input coupling capacitor due to the large pulse of current that flows at switch-on. This can have a magnetising effect on something like a tape head, which can eventually impair its performance to a significant degree. Simply using a low value capacitor is unacceptable as it results in an inadequate bass response. This type of input circuit provides a suitably low input impedance, but it enables a relatively low value input coupling capacitor to be used. In this case the coupling capacitor (C2) has a value of only 470n, but it provides an excellent low frequency response.

The voltage gain provided by IC1 is quite high, varying from about 33 times at high frequencies, to something over 1000 times at the lowest audio frequencies. Despite this high gain, the output level from IC1 is too low to drive most power amplifiers, etc., properly. IC2 is used as an inverting amplifier which has a closed loop voltage gain of about 15 times, and with most cassette tape heads this gives an output level of around one volt r.m.s.

The TLE2037C specified for IC1 is a very low noise operational amplifier which has a noise figure of just 2.5 nanovolts per root hertz. It is internally compensated for closed loop voltage gains of more than 5, which makes it "safe" for this circuit where its minimum gain is about 33 times. Incidentally, the TLE2027C is the fully internally compensated version of the TLE2037C. The signal to noise ratio of the amplifier is good enough to ensure that tape noise will be the main source

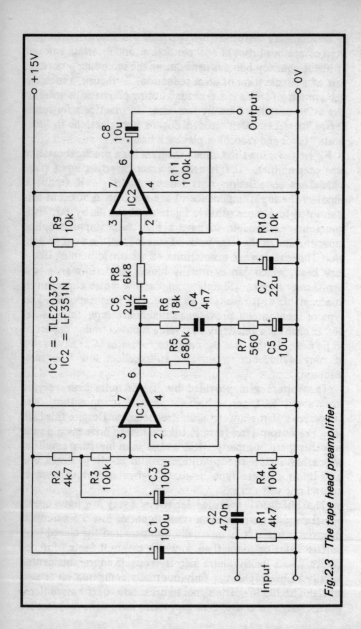

Fig.2.3 The tape head preamplifier

of the noise on the output signal. The distortion level is negligible.

Although it might seem to be worthwhile using an ultra low noise operational amplifier for IC2 as well, the noise performance of IC2 is far less critical than that of IC1. This is due to the fact that IC2 is operating at a relatively low closed loop gain, and with a much higher input level. The noise of IC2 tends to be drowned by the noise received from IC1. However, if the ultimate in performance is required, a lower noise device should be used in the IC2 position.

It is also possible to obtain slightly better noise performance by having the equalised stage at the output of the circuit, and the straightforward amplifier at the input. All the noise generated by the amplifier is then subjected to the lowpass filtering, which minimises high frequency "hiss". In practice this does not usually make a great deal of difference. This is again due to the fact that the output amplifier of the configuration used in Figure 2.3 does not contribute much of the output noise, and subjecting its noise to the lowpass filtering of the equalisation will therefore have little effect on the signal to noise ratio.

Microphone Preamplifier

Low impedance dynamic microphones (plus certain other types which have similar output characteristics) provide a signal level that is very low. In fact it is comparable to a low impedance tape head at about 200 microvolts or so. Obtaining good noise performance with a low impedance microphone is rather more difficult than with a tape head, because no equalisation is required with a microphone. Consequently, a high level of voltage gain is required right up to the 20kHz upper limit of the audio band, giving a relatively large amount of high frequency "hiss". Even so, using a good quality operational amplifier it is possible to obtain a very respectable signal to noise ratio.

The low impedance microphone preamplifier circuit of Figure 2.4 is really just a slightly rearranged version of the tape head preamplifier. The input impedance is a bit lower, and the input stage has no equalisation. Its closed loop voltage gain is about 100 times (40dB), and there is a further

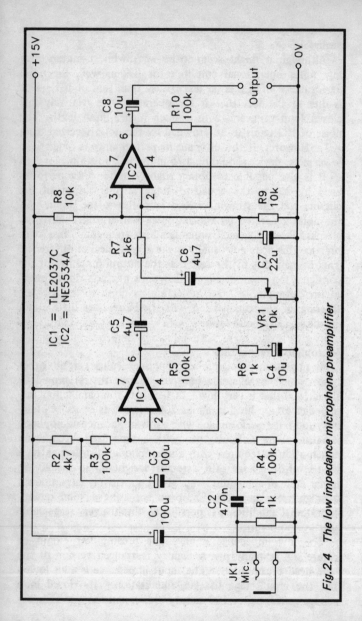

Fig.2.4 The low impedance microphone preamplifier

voltage gain of about 18 times (25dB) provided by IC2. This gives a total voltage gain of well over 60dB, which will provide an output level of over 500 millivolts r.m.s. with most microphones. Output levels vary considerably from one microphone to another, and the way in which a microphone is used also produces wide variations in the output level. If necessary, higher voltage gain can be produced by making R10 higher in value. The circuit includes a gain control (VR1), and this can be used to tame excessive output levels.

Despite the fact that this preamplifier has a high level of voltage gain and a flat frequency response, the signal to noise ratio is quite good. Over the audio range the output noise level is well under one millivolt r.m.s., which gives an unweighted signal to noise ratio of around 60 to 70dB. I used an NE5534A for IC2, but as explained previously, a Bifet device such as the LF351N will give quite good results in the second stage of a low noise preamplifier.

Filters

Operational amplifiers are the standard choice as the basis of most audio filters. In many cases the operational amplifier is used as nothing more than a buffer amplifier in an active filter. For example, the top cut filter of Figure 2.5 is a third order (18dB per octave) type of conventional design. The cutoff frequency is about 6 to 7kHz, making it suitable for use as a scratch filter. IC1b is the buffer amplifier on which the filter is based, while IC1a operates as a buffer stage at the input. The input buffer stage ensures that the main filter circuit is fed from a suitably low source impedance.

Even the 741C has a high level of audio performance when used at unity voltage gain. The 741C is therefore suitable for many filter applications. If something rather better than a 741C is called for, then a Bifet device such as a TLO81C or an LF351N is the obvious choice. In super-fi applications, or any other application where the highest possible level of performance is required, a high quality bipolar operational amplifier can be used.

An NE5532 (or NE5532A) is used in the circuit of Figure 2.5, and this is a good choice if very high performance is needed. These days it is only fractionally more expensive

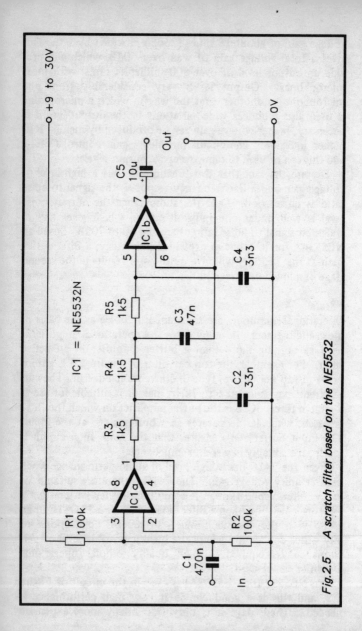

Fig. 2.5 A scratch filter based on the NE5532

+9 to 30V

0V

Out

C5 10u

7

IC1b

5

6

C4 3n3

NE5532N

IC1 = NE5532N

R5 1k5

C3 47n

R4 1k5

C2 33n

R3 1k5

8

IC1a

1

4

3

2

R1 100k

R2 100k

C1 470n

In

than dual Bifet operational amplifiers, and it offers a very high level of audio performance. The gain bandwidth product is 10MHz, the output noise is no more than a few microvolts when it is used as a voltage follower, and the distortion level is negligible. Both the amplifiers in an NE5532 are fully internally compensated, which is an important factor for most filter applications. There are exceptions, but most audio filters have unity gain at some frequencies, and must therefore be based on a fully compensated operational amplifier.

The crosstalk performance of most dual operational amplifiers is quite good, and is adequate for operation with the two amplifiers in different stereo channels. The NE5532 has a crosstalk figure of 110dB at 1kHz, which together with its other excellent performance figures, makes it well suited to use in very high quality stereo equipment. The circuit of Figure 2.6 is for an active tone control circuit based on the NE5532 or NE5532A. This is for one channel of a stereo circuit. The circuit for the other channel is identical, but uses the other section of the NE5532A. All the other components are duplicated in the other channel. Of course, VR1 and VR2 are dual gang components, with one gang being used in each stereo channel. This circuit provides about 12dB or so of boost and cut at 100Hz and 10kHz. Maximum cut is obtained with the wipers at the tops of the tracks — maximum boost is produced with the wipers at the bottom ends of the tracks.

Although the NE5532A offers a crosstalk figure of 110dB, this is not to say that a practical stereo circuit based on the NE5532A will achieve the same degree of isolation between channels. The component layout and wiring must be carefully designed to minimise stray coupling if really good stereo separation is required.

Some audio filters operate at quite high voltage gains, and can be quite noisy if they are based on a 741C or similar "bog standard" device. The audio c.w. (Morse code) filter circuit of Figure 2.7 is an example of a filter which provides a high level of voltage gain. The centre frequency of this bandpass filter is about 900Hz. IC1 just acts as an input buffer stage. The filtering is provided by IC2, which is used as the basis of two conventional bandpass filters. For Morse code reception a fairly narrow bandwidth is sufficient, since there is only one

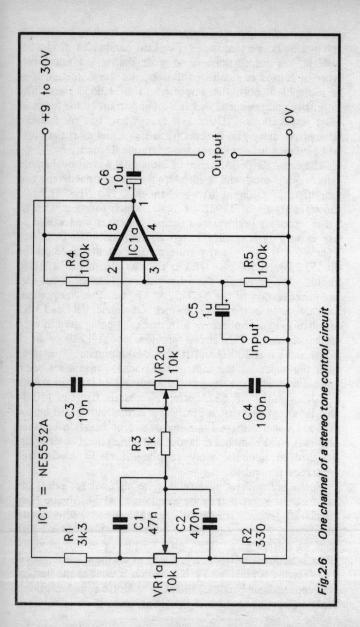

Fig.2.6 One channel of a stereo tone control circuit

74

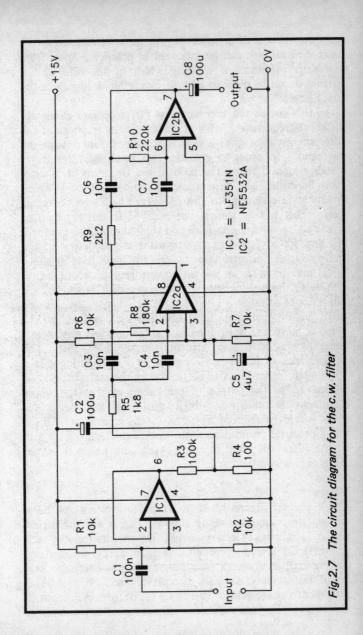

Fig.2.7 The circuit diagram for the c.w. filter

frequency that is of interest. On the other hand, using a very narrow bandwidth can be awkward in practice. Apart from any drift problems, if the bandwidth of the filter is too narrow it can be difficult to tune in any Morse signals in the first place!

In this circuit the two bandpass filters operate at slightly different frequencies. This broadens out the response of the filter slightly, but gives a very rapid roll-off rate outside the passband. In order to give the two bandpass filter stages suitably high Q values the ratio of the two filter resistances must be quite high. In this case the ratio is 100 to 1, which gives a good response but also produces a high level of voltage gain. This voltage gain is not required in this application, where unity voltage gain is all that would normally be needed. R3 and R4 are used as an attenuator at the output of the buffer stage. The attenuator reduces the input level by about 60dB and provides an overall voltage gain of about unity.

Due to the high combined voltage gain of IC2a and IC2b, a fair amount of noise is generated by these two stages. Using a high quality dual operational amplifier such as the NE5532 helps to keep the noise level to a minimum, and gives something like a 20dB improvement over the LM1458C. The performance of IC1 is less important as it is operating with a very much higher input level. In theory the attenuator could be moved to the output of the circuit so that the whole circuit would operate at a high signal level, and the output noise would be reduced by 60dB by the attenuator. This is not a practical proposition though, since the high voltage gain of the filter will result in severe overloading unless the input signal is greatly attenuated.

Mixers

The circuit of Figure 2.8 is for an audio mixer which has a conventional summing mode circuit. This is a mono mixer, but it is merely necessary to use two circuits (one in each channel) for stereo operation. It is primarily designed for mixing high level signals from sources such as electronic keyboard instruments, compact disc players, etc. It provides a maximum voltage gain of two times (6dB) from each input to the output. For use with microphones a suitable preamplifier

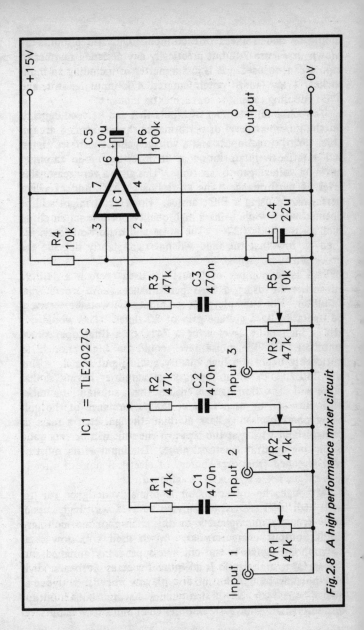

Fig.2.8 A high performance mixer circuit

IC1 = TLE2027C

should be added ahead of each input. Only three inputs are shown in Figure 2.8, but practically any designed number of inputs can be used. It is just a matter of including an input socket, 47k "fader" potentiometer, 47k input resistor, and 470n coupling capacitor for each extra input.

The maximum number of inputs that can be used depends on the minimum level of performance that is deemed acceptable. With three inputs and a voltage gain of just two times, IC1 is effectively operating as an inverting mode amplifier having a voltage gain of six times. This gives a very reasonable level of performance using an ordinary 741C, and excellent performance using a Bifet device. However, it might still be deemed worthwhile using a high quality operational amplifier such as the TLE2027C. The noise and distortion levels are then so low that the unit will not significantly degrade the processed audio signals.

If a large number of inputs are used there is a definite advantage in using a high performance audio operational amplifier. For example, with ten inputs IC1 would effectively be operating at a voltage gain of 20 times. This would not give a high noise level using a 741C or a Bifet operational amplifier, but the noise level could be high enough to noticeably degrade a high quality audio input signal. Using the TLE2027C, or an operational amplifier having similar noise and distortion figures, ensures that a substantial number of inputs can be used without the performance of the unit being compromised. Bear in mind though, that a mass of controls and wiring at the input of the unit will be very good at picking up stray electrical noise. The input wiring must be well screened from any sources of electrical noise if a really low output noise level is to be achieved.

Although the mixer circuit is primarily designed for use with high level signals, it can also be used with high impedance dynamic microphones, or any microphones which have similar output characteristics. When used with low level microphone signals it will not give super-fi performance, but the signal to noise ratio is adequate for many purposes. It is also possible to use the mixer with low impedance dynamic microphones, or any microphones having similar output characteristics. However, in order to obtain a reasonable level

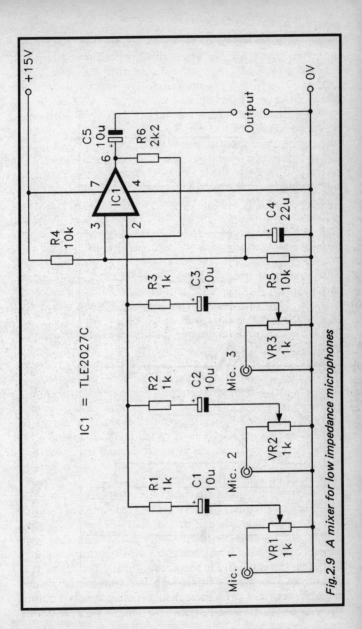

Fig.2.9 A mixer for low impedance microphones

79

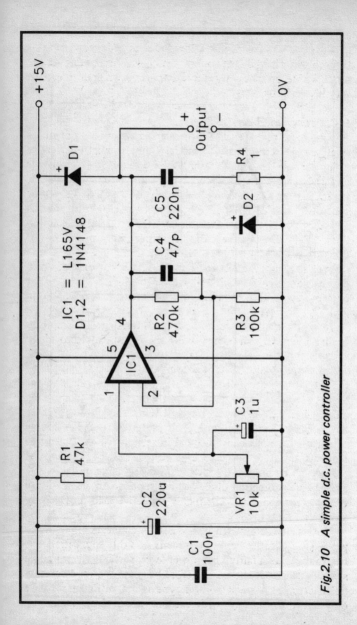

Fig.2.10 A simple d.c. power controller

of performance it is best to use the slightly modified circuit of Figure 2.9. This is just a low input impedance version of the original circuit. Of course, really good screening of the input wiring becomes even more important when dealing with very low-level signals.

D.C. Power Controllers

The main use of d.c. power controllers is as a speed control for small d.c. electric motors (model trains, miniature electric drills, etc.). At its most basic level a d.c. power controller is just a variable voltage source having a low output impedance. Figure 2.10 shows the circuit diagram for a simple d.c. power controller which is intended for use with small 12 volt electric motors. The circuit is based on an L165V operational amplifier. Physically this device looks rather like a plastic power transistor, but it has five "legs" not three, and it is a true operational amplifier. It can handle output currents of up to 4 amps, and has a supply voltage range of 12 to 36 volts (or plus and minus 6 to 18 volts). Its maximum power dissipation figure is 20 watts.

In this circuit it is used as a non-inverting d.c. amplifier having a voltage gain of just under six times. VR1 provides a variable input voltage that enables the output potential to be varied from about 1 volt to around 13 volts. Although the output voltage can not be set to less than one volt, and the motor connected across the output will always be consuming a certain amount of power, one volt is insufficient to turn-over any normal 12 volt d.c. motor. If preferred though, a couple of silicon rectifiers can be added in series with the output to reduce the output potential by a volt or so. C4, C5, and R4 are needed to prevent the circuit from becoming unstable. D1 and D2 are protection diodes which suppress any high voltage spikes generated across the highly inductive load provided by an electric motor.

Note that the heat-tab of the L165V connects internally to pin 3 (the negative supply terminal). In this application IC1 has to dissipate a fairly high power level, particularly at middle speed settings. It should therefore be mounted on a substantial heatsink. A small bolt-on type is not sufficient. I have only tried the circuit with motors which draw maximum currents of about 1 amp or so, but the circuit should work with motors which consume a maximum current of 2 amps. The circuit should be powered from a reasonably stable 15 volt supply, and the supply circuit should incorporate current limiting at a suitable level for the motor that will be driven from unit. A 15 volt monolithic voltage regulator is the obvious basis for the power supply unit.

Pulsed Controller

Pulsed controllers provide improved results with d.c. electric motors, especially at slow speeds. Motors tend to stall at slow speeds when powered from a simple variable voltage controller. The circuit diagram of Figure 2.11 is for a very simple but effective pulsed power controller.

It is based on a basic operational amplifier astable circuit. However, steering diodes D1 and D2, plus potentiometer VR1 are included in the timing circuit. C3 charges via D2, R4, and the lower section of VR1. It discharges through D1, R4, and the upper section of VR1. With VR1 at a middle setting a 1 : 1 mark-space ratio is obtained at the output, and the average output voltage is about half the supply potential. Moving the wiper of VR1 further up its track gives a longer charge time and a shorter discharge time. The mark-space ratio of the output signal therefore becomes higher, as does the average output voltage. Moving the wiper down the track has the opposite effect, with the average output voltage being reduced.

VR1 therefore permits the average output voltage to be varied from a low level to about 12 volts or so, permitting a full range of motor speeds to be produced. Although this is a pulsed type controller, IC1 still has to dissipate a significant amount of power. It should therefore be fitted on a medium sized heatsink. Like the previous circuit, this one provides a minimum output potential of one volt. This is unlikely to be of any practical importance, but a pair of silicon rectifiers connected in series with the output can be used to provide a reduction of just over a volt in the output potential. The circuit should be powered from a reasonably smooth and stable 15 volt supply which should include current limiting. The output frequency is about 100Hz, which should give good results with most motors. However, the output frequency is easily changed by altering the

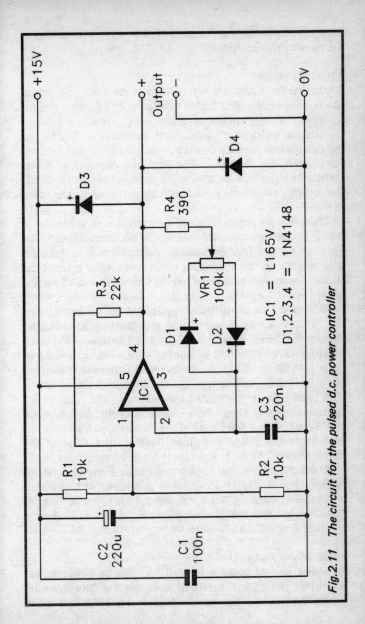

Fig.2.11 The circuit for the pulsed d.c. power controller

value of C3. The output frequency is inversely proportional to the value of this component.

P.W.M. Controller
A pulse width modulator can be used as the basis of a pulsed power controller. The circuit of Figure 2.12 is for a p.w.m. equivalent to the circuit of Figure 2.11. This is a conventional pulse width modulator circuit, but using an L165V for the comparator permits a suitable electric motor to be driven direct from the output. The oscillator operates at about 100Hz, but this can be altered by changing the value of C2. The output frequency is inversely proportional to the value of C2.

The main advantage of using a proper p.w.m. controller is that it is voltage controlled. Although the control voltage for the circuit is provided by a simple potentiometer in this case, it is possible to use something more elaborate to control the circuit. A control voltage of between about 0 and 13 volts is needed at pin 1 of IC2.

In a model train controller application the control voltage can be provided by a circuit that provides simulated inertia, momentum, and braking. Figure 2.13 shows a circuit which gives this method of control. This circuit is used in place of VR1 in the main circuit. VR1 is the speed control, but C – R delay circuits prevent any changes in the setting of VR1 from being implemented immediately. The value of R1 controls the delay time of the simulated inertia, and the value of R2 controls the delay time of the simulated momentum. In both cases the delays are proportional to the value of the timing resistor. S1 is the emergency brake control.

Another possible means of control is to derive the control voltage from a digital to analogue converter, with the controller being operated via a computer. This type of thing is useful for general robotics applications, as well as computer controlled model train layouts.

Audio Power Amps.
Although not designed specifically for use in audio power amplifiers, the L165V seems to work quite well in this role. Figure 2.14 shows the circuit diagram for a Class B audio

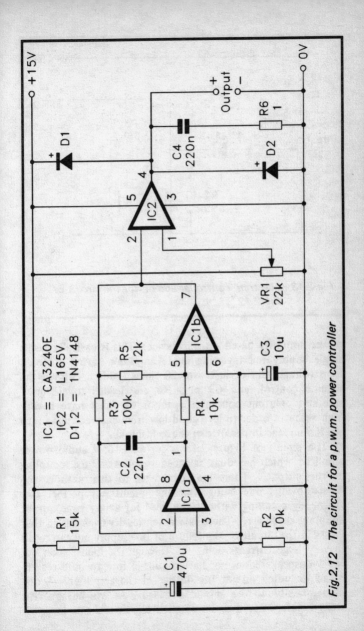

Fig.2.12 The circuit for a p.w.m. power controller

85

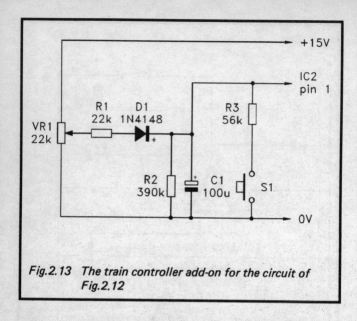

Fig.2.13 The train controller add-on for the circuit of Fig.2.12

power amplifier based on this device. This is basically just a single supply rail inverting mode amplifier having a closed loop voltage gain of just over 20 times (26dB). VR1 is the volume control, and C3 plus R4 are needed to aid good stability. Output coupling capacitor C4 must have a very high value in order to give good low frequency coupling into the 8 ohm load impedance of the loudspeaker.

The circuit of Figure 2.15 is for an L165V audio power amplifier which has dual balanced supplies and d.c. coupling at the output. There are advantages to this method, the most obvious one being that the circuit has perfect low frequency coupling without the need for a very large output coupling capacitor. There is a potential disadvantage in that faults in the circuit or the failure of one supply rail can result in very large currents being fed through the loudspeaker. If the loudspeaker does not have a built-in fuse I would recommend including one at the output of the amplifier. A one amp quick-blow fuse should be used. As will be apparent from Figure 2.15, the d.c. coupled circuit is a non-inverting

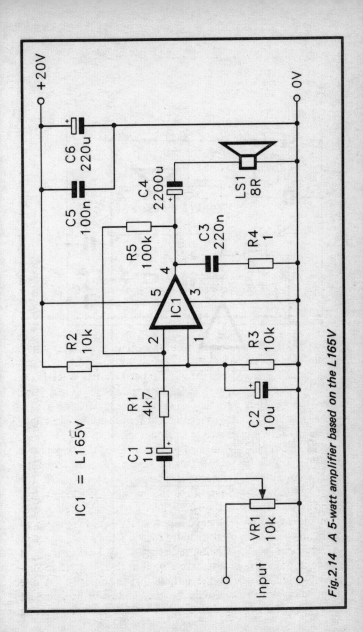

Fig.2.14 A 5-watt amplifier based on the L165V

IC1 = L165V

87

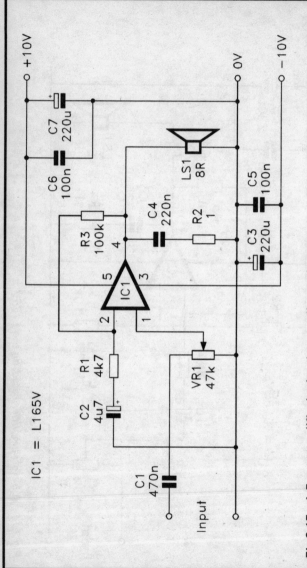

Fig. 2.15 A 5-watt amplifier having d.c. coupling at the output

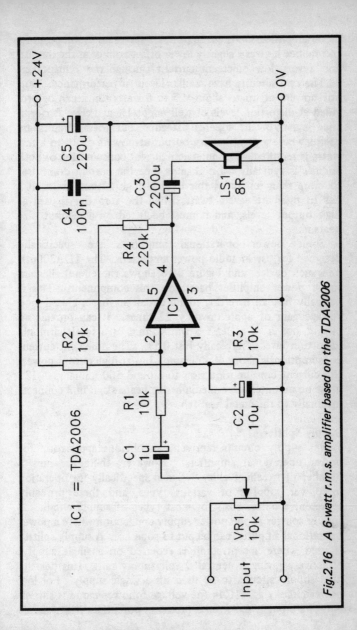

Fig.2.16 A 6-watt r.m.s. amplifier based on the TDA2006

IC1 = TDA2006

+24V

0V

C5 220u

C4 100n

C3 2200u

R4 220k

IC1

R2 10k

R3 10k

R1 10k

C2 10u

C1 1u

VR1 10k

Input

LS1 8R

89

mode amplifier. On the face of it, C2 serves no useful purpose. In practice it gives a slightly lower offset voltage at the output, and a very low quiescent current through the loudspeaker.

The two circuits have similar levels of performance. Output powers of up to about 4.5 to 5 watts r.m.s. can be provided at distortion levels of well under 1% at 1kHz. Performance is not in the super-fi category, but these circuits are useful where a good quality output at powers of up to a few watts is required. The quiescent current consumption of both circuits is typically 40 milliamps, but the current drain rises to more than ten times this level at high output levels. IC1 has to dissipate several watts when the amplifier is used at high output levels, and it must be fitted on a medium size heatsink.

Some power operational amplifiers are specifically designed for use in audio power amplifiers. The TDA2006 is one such device, and Figure 2.16 shows the circuit diagram for a power amplifier based on this component. This is basically just an inverting mode circuit having a closed loop voltage gain of approximately 22 times. It can provide an output power of at least 6 watts r.m.s. at a total harmonic distortion level of typically just 0.1%. The quiescent current consumption is about 40 milliamps, but at high output powers the current consumption rises to around 500 milliamps. IC1 must be mounted on a medium size heatsink. Pin 3 connects internally to the metal heat-tab.

Supply Splitter

Power supply circuits represent an obvious application for power operational amplifiers. However, there are now a number of excellent chips designed specifically for operation in power supplies of various types, and these probably represent a better basis for most types of supply circuit. A supply splitter is one power supply application where a power operational amplifier can be put to good use. A supply splitter is used where a centre tap is required on a single supply, effectively giving a central 0 volt supply rail. This permits dual supply circuits to be used on a single supply. For low power circuits a 741C in the voltage follower mode is sufficient. Its input is fed from a precision potential divider circuit which generates an accurate half supply voltage bias signal. The output of the 741C then provides the artificial centre tap on the supply.

The L165V can be used in much the same way in applications where output currents of more than a few milliamps are required. The L165V can be used as a supply splitter with output currents of up to a few hundred milliamps. Figure 2.17 shows the circuit diagram for an L165V supply splitter. R2 and R3 should have a tolerance rating of 1% or better. At a.c. the circuit has a voltage gain of about 20 times. This may seem to be pointless, but the L165V seems to have much better stability when used in this way. Of course, due to the inclusion of C1 the closed loop voltage gain is unity at d.c., and the correct output voltage is produced.

The power dissipated by IC1 obviously depends on the supply voltage and output current levels. Even if it is used at output currents of only about 50 milliamps it will probably have to be fitted with a small bolt-on heatsink. Output current significantly beyond 50 milliamps will require the use of a more substantial heatsink.

P.W.M. Audio
The basics of pulse width modulation were fully discussed in Chapter 1. Figures 2.18 and 2.19 show the circuit diagram for a pulse width modulator that can be used to feed an audio signal through an opto-isolator. Figure 2.18 shows the circuit for the modulator section of the system. This is a conventional circuit which operates at a frequency of about 65kHz. R6 and R7 provide biasing at the input of the modulator. No input filter is used, and with a clock frequency of 65kHz there will probably be no need to remove frequencies close to the clock frequency. However, if the unit is used with an input signal which might have a significant high frequency content, lowpass filtering must be used prior to feeding the signal to the input of the modulator.

I used an LF353N for IC1, but practically any fast dual operational amplifier will give good results. On trying various devices in the IC2 position the CA3140E seemed to give the best output waveform. Many other fast operational amplifiers will give good results though. There is no point in using

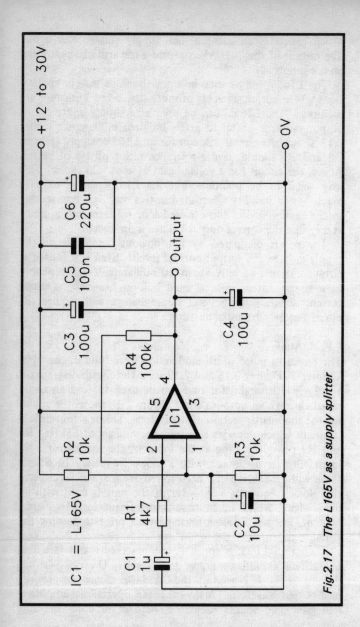

Fig. 2.17 The L165V as a supply splitter

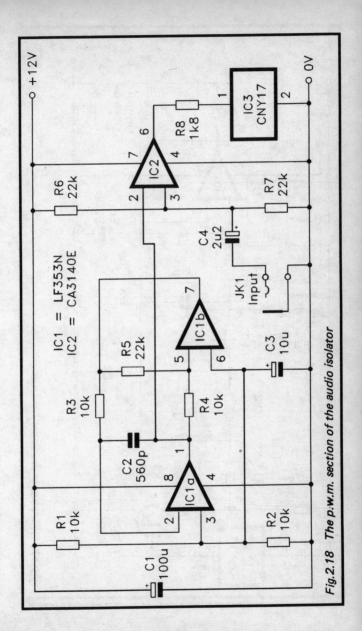

Fig.2.18 The p.w.m. section of the audio isolator

93

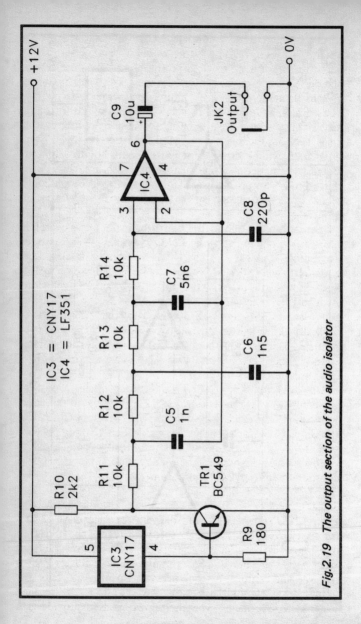

Fig. 2.19 The output section of the audio isolator

94

ultra-fast operational amplifiers in the modulator and comparator stages. Although this would give a better output waveform from IC2, it would not have a significant effect on the performance of the unit as a whole. The weak link in the system is the opto-isolator. Opto-isolators are not particularly fast devices, and most are too slow for this application. High speed types which have a built-in common emitter output stage (6N139, etc.) give quite good results. The CNY17 plus a discrete switching transistor (TR1) seems to give a slightly faster switching time though, together with a slightly lower noise level. Surprisingly perhaps, most of the output noise seems to be contributed by the opto-isolator, and not by the modulator.

The output section of the unit is basically just a switching transistor and a fourth order (24dB per octave) lowpass filter. The cutoff frequency of the latter is at about 10kHz. This gives quite good results, but the clock frequency of 65kHz is high enough to provide the full 20kHz audio bandwidth. Reducing R11 to R14 to a value of 4k7 provides the full audio bandwidth, but it also gives a relatively high level of clock breakthrough at the output. This could be corrected by using another fourth order filter to give further attenuation of the clock signal. This would give almost 80dB of clock suppression.

Obviously the modulator and output circuits must be powered from separate supplies so that there is no direct connection between the two circuits via the supply rails. The circuit can comfortably handle input levels of several volts peak to peak. In order to obtain a really good signal to noise ratio the unit should be used with an input signal level of around two to five volts peak-to-peak.

Signal Generator

Figure 2.20 shows the circuit diagram for a sinewave generator that covers the full audio spectrum (20Hz to 20kHz) in one range. The circuit has IC1a as a thermistor stabilised Wien oscillator, and IC1b as an output buffer stage. VR2 is the variable output attenuator, and opening S1 cuts the output level by 40dB. Setting low output levels is much easier with S1 open. The thermistor used to provide gain

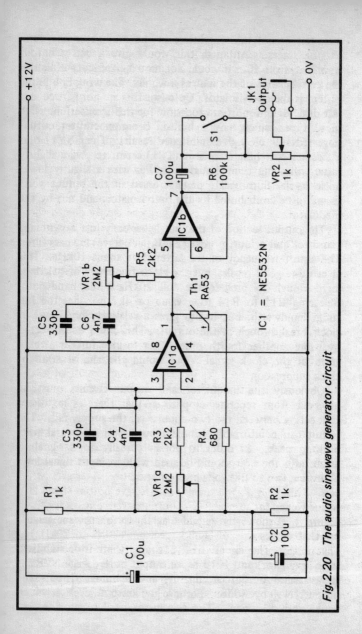

Fig. 2.20 The audio sinewave generator circuit

stabilisation is the RA53, which also seems to be sold as the R53. This is designed specifically for use in circuits such as this, and it gives no significant variation in the output level over the full frequency range covered. The maximum output level is approximately 3 volts peak-to-peak.

Ideally VR1 would be an antilog potentiometer, but a dual gang antilog potentiometer of the correct value will almost certainly be unobtainable. A linear type can be used, but this will give non-linear scaling. Alternatively, a logarithmic potentiometer can be used, but connected in reverse (i.e. clockwise adjustment giving decreased output frequency). This will give more linear scaling, but it is unlikely to give a highly linear scale. The lack of linearity is simply due to the fact that the laws of logarithmic potentiometers are only approximations. This is reflected in the frequency scaling obtained in this application. Anyway, for good accuracy it is best to use a frequency meter when setting the output frequency, rather than relying on a calibrated scale around the control knob of VR1.

Any low noise, low distortion operational amplifiers should give good results in this circuit. The NE5532 is a low cost way of providing two high performance operational amplifiers, but it gives a very high degree of performance. The total noise and distortion on the output should be at about −80dB or less, which is more than adequate for most audio testing.

A squarewave output can be provided using the add-on circuit of Figure 2.21. IC2 operates as a voltage comparator. One input of IC2 is fed with the half supply bias level, while the other is fed with the sinewave output signal from IC1b. The output therefore goes fully positive on positive sinewave half cycles, and fully negative on negative sinewave half cycles. This gives a good quality squarewave output signal at about 9 volts peak-to-peak. The output level controls for the squarewave output are the same as those for the sinewave output.

The device used in the IC2 position needs to be a fast device having a low level of overshoot. The LF356N is a popular choice for applications such as this, but the CA3140E and LF351N were also found to give good results.

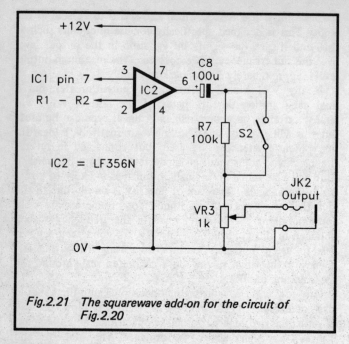

*Fig.2.21   The squarewave add-on for the circuit of
Fig.2.20*

High R Voltmeter

One of the main advantages of digital multimeters over ordinary analogue units is that the digital instruments have much higher input resistances. As a result of this they produce much less loading of the test circuit, and more reliable readings. Of course, it is possible to add an amplifier ahead of an ordinary moving coil meter to give an input resistance which is comparable to that of a digital multimeter. Figure 2.22 shows the circuit diagram for a high resistance voltmeter of this type.

This is an application which does not really merit dual supply rails since the output will always have the same polarity. The circuit is therefore based on a CA3140E which is capable of operating as a single supply d.c. amplifier. It also has a PMOS input stage with an input resistance of over a million megohms. This ensures that there is no significant loading on the input attenuator. The latter is a three step type which provides full scale voltages of 1V, 10V, and 100V. R5 and D1

98

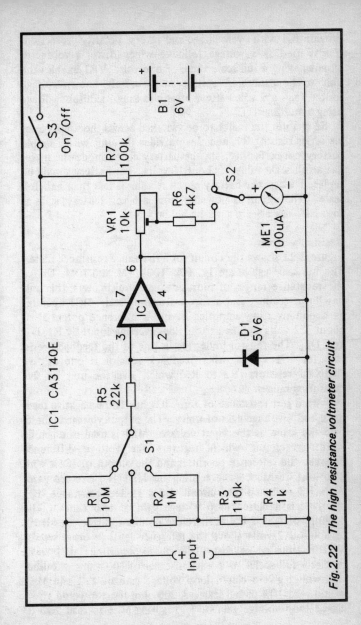

Fig.2.22 *The high resistance voltmeter circuit*

provide IC1 with over-voltage and reverse polarity protection. IC1 is used as a voltage follower which drives a voltmeter circuit having a full scale value of one volt. VR1 enables the unit to be calibrated against an accurately known voltage source (e.g. a 9 volt battery after checking its output voltage using a multimeter).

S2 enables the meter to be switched across the supply lines via series resistor R7, and this provides the unit with a simple battery check facility. In the battery check mode the meter has a full scale value of about 10 volts. The battery should be replaced when the battery check reading is less than half full scale. The circuit is powered from a 6 volt battery, such as four HP7 size cells in a plastic holder.

Resistance Meter

Figure 2.23 shows the circuit for a five range resistance meter. The full scale values are 1k, 10k, 100k, 1M, and 10M. Unlike the resistance ranges of most analogue multimeters, this unit has linear scaling, and a forward reading scale. IC1 operates as a non-inverting amplifier having a reference potential of about 1.2 volts supplied to its non-inverting input by R1, D1, and D2. The resistor under test is one of the feedback resistors for IC1. The other feedback resistor is one of five switched resistors (R2 to R6) which give the unit its five measuring ranges.

With a test resistance of zero, IC1 has 100% negative feedback and a voltage gain of unity. The output voltage is therefore the same as the input voltage. ME1 is used in a simple voltmeter circuit which registers the voltage difference between the reference potential and the output of IC1. With zero test resistance the reading on ME1 is therefore zero. With R2 switched into circuit and a 1k test resistance, IC1 clearly has a closed loop voltage gain of two times. The output voltage of IC1 is therefore double the reference level, or about 1.2 volts above the reference level in other words. VR1 is adjusted so that under these conditions ME1 reads precisely full scale. If a test resistance of 100 ohms was used, this would give a closed loop voltage gain of 1.1, and ME1 would read 10% of full scale. A 200 ohm resistor would give a closed loop voltage gain of 1.2, causing ME1 to read 20% of

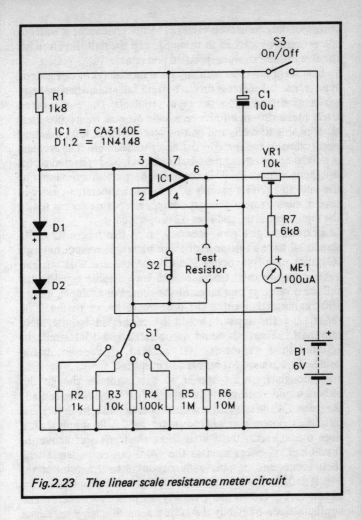

Fig.2.23   The linear scale resistance meter circuit

full scale.

It should be apparent from this that the circuit provides the desired action, with the deflection of ME1's pointer being proportional to the value of the test resistance. ME1 can therefore be scaled directly in terms of resistance, and there is no difficulty in converting readings on its 0 to 100 scale into corresponding resistance values. The full scale value is equal to the resistance switched in using S1, and the unit therefore has the five full scale values specified previously.

One slight problem with any resistance meter of this general type is that the meter is driven beyond full scale when no resistor is connected across the input terminals. The unit is effectively measuring an infinite resistance. Most moving coil meters are well able to withstand quite severe overloads, but prolonged overloading of the meter is definitely undesirable. The problem is overcome by having push-button switch S2 connected across the input terminals. This normally short circuits the input of the unit and gives a reading of zero on the meter. In order to take a measurement the test component is first connected to the input terminals, and then S2 is operated.

In order to give good accuracy on all five ranges R2 to R6 should all have a tolerance of 1% or better. A resistor having a tolerance of 1% or better is also needed for calibration purposes. Ideally this resistor should have a value equal to the full scale value of one range of the unit. For example, using a 100k calibration resistor the unit would be set to the 100k range, and the resistor would be connected to the input terminals. Then S2 would be operated and VR1 would be adjusted for a reading of "100" on ME1. It does not matter which range is used for calibration purposes.

Although it might appear at first sight as though this circuit would work properly using a 741C, this is not actually the case. Although IC1 does not operate with its inputs and output at potentials right down to the 0 volt supply rail, it does operate with them little more than one volt above the 0 volt rail. Devices such as the 741C can not operate with their inputs and outputs within about 2 to 2.5 volts of the 0 volt rail, and would therefore fail to work properly in this circuit. A 741C could probably be made to work on this configuration, but only by using a much higher reference voltage that would keep the inputs and output above their minimum operating levels. The CA3140E is probably a better choice anyway, since it has a PMOS input stage which draws negligible input currents. This ensures that there is no loss of accuracy on the highest range where very high value feedback resistances are involved.

102

Current Tracker

A current tracker is a device which is used to check the current flowing through printed circuit tracks. This can only be done with an ordinary multimeter if the track is broken, and the meter is connected across the break in the track. The most sophisticated current trackers use expensive Hall effect sensors to detect the small magnetic field generated by the current passing through the track. Inexpensive trackers (such as the ones featured here) are really just very sensitive voltmeters which measure the small voltage drop through a length of track. This voltage drop is not very large, since the resistance through a small piece of track is only a few milliohms, and the current flow may well be no more than a few milliamps. The current tracker must therefore respond to input voltages that will often be just a few microvolts.

Figure 2.24 shows the circuit diagram for a simple current tracker based on a CA3140E. This is basically just a single supply d.c. amplifier which drives a voltmeter circuit. The voltmeter has a full scale value of about one volt, and the closed loop voltage gain of IC1 is about 300 times. An input voltage of just over three millivolts therefore produces a full scale reading on ME1. S1 and R6 provide a battery checking facility. R2 and D1 provide over-voltage protection at the input of the circuit.

Although the circuit of Figure 2.24 is quite sensitive, it does not have sufficient gain to track down very small current flows. R4 can be made lower in value in order to obtain increased voltage gain, but in practice this is unlikely to give good results. Input offset voltages are almost certain to result in the output drifting strongly positive, or in small input voltages failing to produce a change in the output voltage.

Improved Current Tracker

For high d.c. voltage gains a precision operational amplifier having very low offset voltages is needed. The OP-07C is popular for precision d.c. applications, but there are now various alternatives which offer even higher performance. The current tracker of Figure 2.25 is based on one of these, the OP-77GP. Some of the parameters of this device are something less than impressive. For example, its gain bandwidth

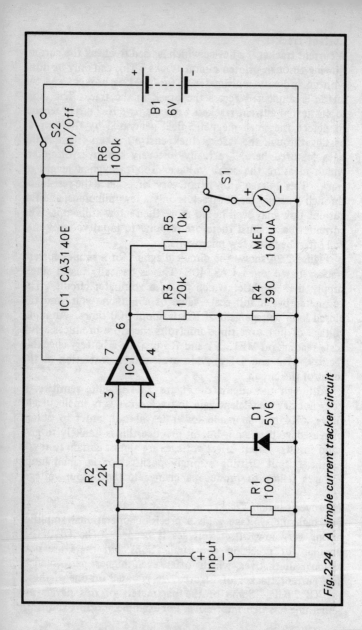

Fig. 2.24 A simple current tracker circuit

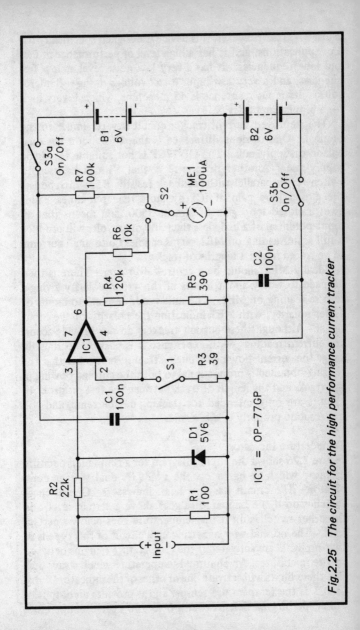

Fig.2.25   The circuit for the high performance current tracker

is just 3.4kHz. However, this device is designed specifically for d.c. applications, and it has a high level of performance at d.c. and low frequencies. It has a very low noise level at low frequencies, and a very low input offset voltage rating (60 microvolts). Its input resistance is 45 megohms, which is very high for a bipolar input device.

The improved current tracker circuit is very similar to the original. One obvious difference is that this circuit has dual balanced supply rails. The OP-77GP is not suitable for single supply use. Another difference is that S1 can be used to switch R3 in parallel with feedback resistor R5, which boosts the closed loop gain of IC1 by more than ten times. This gives a closed loop gain of almost 3500, and means that an input potential of a little less than 300 microvolts will produce a full scale reading on ME1. This enables quite small currents to be traced in short lengths of track.

Ideally ME1 should be a centre-zero meter. There is then no need to worry about inputs of the wrong polarity giving a reverse reading on ME1. The unit would respond to inputs of either polarity, with ME1 indicating the polarity of the input signal. Although these current trackers do not provide accurate current readings, with experience it is possible to roughly gauge the current flowing through a track. Remember that the reading obtained is proportional to both the current flowing in the track, and the length of track between the test prods. Both circuits are only intended for tracking d.c. currents, and will not respond properly to a.c. signals.

Temperature Indicator
Figure 2.26 shows the circuit diagram for a simple temperature monitor which is based on the LM393N dual voltage comparator. The circuit has two l.e.d. indicators. One of these switches on if the temperature goes above a certain level, and the other switches on if the temperature goes below a certain level. The normal way of setting up a circuit of this type is so that no lights are activated if the temperature remains between two temperatures. An abnormal temperature which strays outside these limits will activate one or other of the indicator l.e.d.s.

IC1 is the temperature sensor, and it provides an output of 10mV per degree Celcius over a 0 to 100 degree temperature

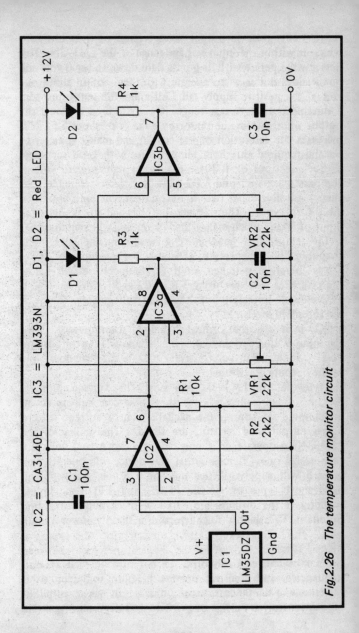

Fig.2.26 The temperature monitor circuit

range. This gives an output voltage range of 0 to one volt, which is within the input voltage range of the LM393N. This device will operate with its inputs right down to the 0 volt rail, but it does not seem to operate with them within about one volt of the positive supply rail. Although the sensor provides a suitable output voltage range, IC2 is still used to boost the output voltage from the sensor by a factor of about 5.5. This increases the resolution of the circuit, and makes it easier to set the required threshold temperatures with good accuracy.

Both sections of IC3 are used as straightforward voltage comparators. VR1 and VR2 provide variable reference voltages. Ideally these two preset potentiometers should be multi-turn types. The output of IC2 is fed to the inverting input of IC3a, which means that its output will switch on D1 if the temperature goes above a level set using VR1. The output of IC2 connects to the non-inverting input of IC3b. D2 is therefore switched on if the temperature falls below the reference level set using VR2. C2 and C3 are needed to ensure stable operation with the input voltage close to one of the threshold levels.

IC3 is acting as a form of "window" discriminator. With the input within certain limits (the "window") the outputs are "off". If the input voltage strays outside the "window" one of the outputs is activated.

Note that the LM393N, like most other voltage comparators, has open collector outputs. These can sink up to 50 milliamps. Of course, the available source current is zero unless output load resistors are fitted. The ability of the LM393N to operate on supply voltages down to 2 volts is a very useful one. It means that this device will operate well on a 5 volt supply. When used on a 5 volt supply it will drive most types on CMOS, PMOS, and TTL logic inputs properly if the outputs are fitted with 1k pull-up resistors (standard TTL inputs might require a slightly lower value).

Video Fader

Normal operational amplifiers do not operate well at high frequencies, and can not provide medium to high output currents. This renders them unusable in video amplifier applications, where input frequencies up to several megahertz are involved, and outputs must drive 75 ohm loads with signal levels of a few volts peak-to-peak. However, there are some operational amplifiers which are designed specifically for use in video applications. These include the EL2020C which is optimised for gains between −10 and +10 times, and is capable of driving two standard video inputs. The EL2001C is a useful device for video applications, but I suppose that strictly speaking it is not an operational amplifier. It has 100% negative feedback via an internal feedback circuit which means that it can only operate as a unity voltage gain buffer amplifier. However, this is all that is required in many video applications.

Figure 2.27 shows the circuit diagram for a simple video fader based on the EL2001C. This is used at the output of a simple fader circuit of the clipping type. As the wiper of VR1 is moved down its track the positive part of the video signal (the luminance signal) is progressively clipped. Eventually it is removed altogether, leaving only the synchronisation signal. VR2 is adjusted to give optimum fading with VR1 fully backed-off.

The EL2001C has a −3dB point at 70MHz, and its quiescent current consumption is only 1.4 milliamps. It no doubt has many applications outside the video field.

Audio mV Meter

The circuit for a very simple audio millivolt meter is shown in Figure 2.28. This has three ranges with full scale values of 10 millivolts, 100 millivolts, and 1 volt r.m.s. The input impedance is about 110k, and measurements are accurate over the full 20Hz to 20kHz audio range.

A three step attenuator (R1 to R3) is included at the input of the circuit, and this gives the unit its three ranges. The rest of the circuit is basically just a precision full-wave rectifier driving a moving coil meter. Although this circuit is very different to the precision half-wave configuration discussed in Chapter 1, it operates using the same basic principle. The meter is driven via a full-wave bridge rectifier, and by including the rectifier in the negative feedback circuit the amplifier is made to compensate for the non-linearity of the germanium diodes. VR1 is the sensitivity control, and it enables the unit to be calibrated against a known input voltage.

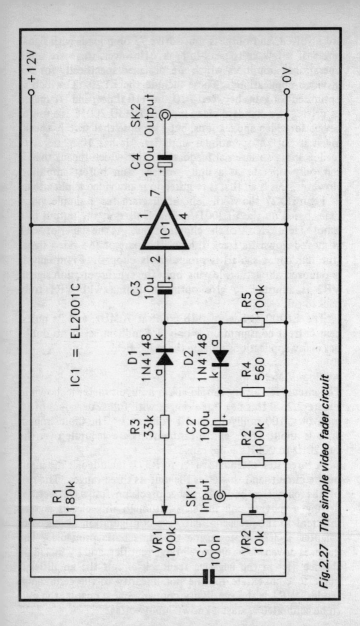

Fig.2.27 The simple video fader circuit

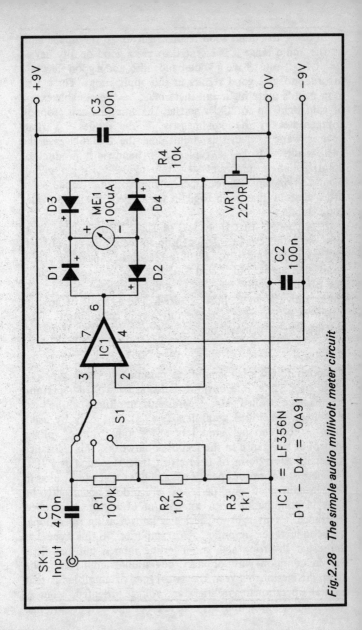

Fig.2.28 The simple audio millivolt meter circuit

111

In order to obtain good results right up to the upper limit of the audio range it is essential to use a good quality device for IC1. It must have a wide bandwidth and a good slew rate in order to give good results in this application. The closed loop gain is quite high, and there must be a reasonable excess of gain right up to 20kHz so that the amplifier can properly compensate for the non-linearity of the diodes. Various devices were tried in this circuit, and the LF356N gave the best results. It has a typical gain bandwidth product of 4.5MHz and a minimum slew rate of 10 volts per microsecond (typically 12 volts per microsecond). Unlike some other devices that were tried in the circuit, it also provides good stability.

It is possible that there will be slight offset voltage problems with this circuit. This can be corrected using an offset-null control. This is just a 10k preset resistor having its track connected across pins 1 and 5 of IC1, and its wiper wired to the positive supply rail. It is simply adjusted to zero the meter with the input short-circuited. There should be no drift problems in this case, because only a very small output offset voltage is being trimmed out.

V.C.A.s

Although operational amplifiers can handle most types of audio processing, one obvious omission from their repertoire is voltage controlled gain. Operational amplifiers can be used in voltage controlled amplifiers (v.c.a.s), but only by using them as conventional amplifiers having some form of voltage controlled resistance in the feedback network. This resistance is usually some form of field effect transistor such as a Jfet.

There is a form of operational amplifier that can be used in voltage controlled amplifiers, and which does not need to be used in conjunction with some form of voltage controlled resistance. This type of device is known as an operational transconductance amplifier. An amplifier of this type has the usual inverting and non-inverting inputs, but has little else in common with ordinary operational amplifiers. The main distinction between the two types of amplifier is that normal operational amplifiers are voltage oriented, whereas transconductance amplifiers deal in input and output currents.

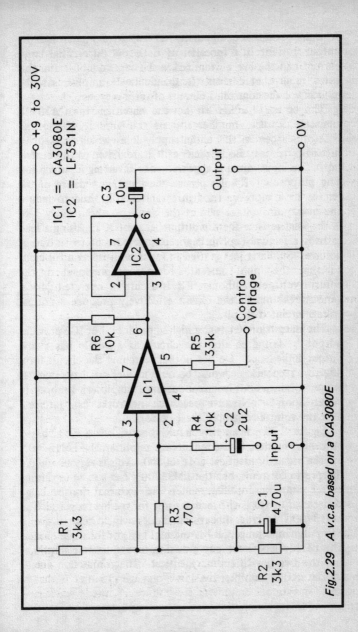

Fig.2.29 A v.c.a. based on a CA3080E

113

A transconductance amplifier has an extra input, and the output current is a function of both the differential input current and the bias current fed to the control input. It is this extra input that enables transconductance amplifiers to be used in voltage controlled circuits of various types.

The circuit diagram for a v.c.a. based on the CA3080E transconductance amplifier appears in Figure 2.29. R1 and R2 form a centre-tap on the supply lines which is used for biasing purposes. Both inputs of IC1 are biased to this centre-tap. The input signal is applied to the inverting input via R4. The purpose of R4 is to raise the input impedance of the circuit to a more useful figure (about 10k), and to reduce the maximum voltage gain of the circuit to about unity. R6 is the load resistor for the output stage of IC1. Using a load resistor effectively converts the output current to an output voltage. Similarly, R5 is used in series with the control input so that the input current becomes proportional to the control voltage. Although IC1 is a current operated device, various resistors in the circuit effectively produce a normal voltage oriented circuit.

The output of IC1 is at a high impedance, but IC2 provides output buffering so that the circuit as a whole has a low output impedance. Do not bother searching the circuit for a negative feedback network, because it does not have one. It is quite normal for transconductance amplifiers to operate "open loop". Negative feedback networks can interfere with the voltage control of these devices.

Figure 2.30 shows the circuit diagram for a v.c.a. based on a more modern transconductance amplifier, the LM13700N (or the virtually identical LM13600N). This is very much like the previous circuit, but the LM31700N has a built-in output buffer amplifier which renders an external buffer stage unnecessary. R8 is the load resistor for the buffer stage. The LM13700N includes linearising diodes which help to give a wider dynamic range. R7 is the bias resistor for these diodes. The LM13700N is actually a dual transconductance amplifier, and the two amplifiers are identical. The connection details for the second amplifier are shown on page 115.

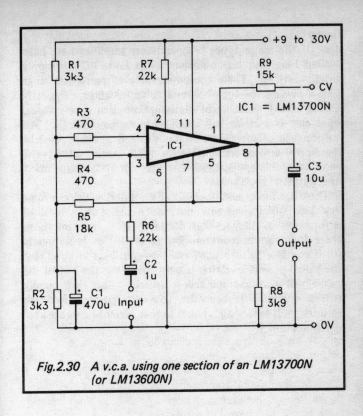

Fig.2.30 *A v.c.a. using one section of an LM13700N (or LM13600N)*

Pin No.	Function	Other Amp. Pin No.
16	Control input	1
15	Diode bias input	2
14	Non-inverting input	3
13	Inverting input	4
12	Output	5
10	Buffer input	7
9	Buffer output	8

115

Finally

Most of the major types of operational amplifier have been covered here, but one omission is the range of low supply current devices. These consume supply currents that range from a few microamps to around 200 microamps. The early devices gave lower current consumptions than conventional types, but as a result had much narrower bandwidths. The performance of some devices also suffered in other respects. These early devices are suitable for use in sensing circuits and many other d.c. applications, but were not suitable for many other practical applications.

There are now some operational amplifiers which consume very low supply currents but which maintain a level of performance similar to that of the 741C. In applications where low current consumption is needed it is definitely worth considering these devices. However, bear in mind that true micro-power operation is only possible if the rest of the circuit will consume minimal currents. Also, low supply current operation is dependent on bias resistors, feedback resistors, etc., having high values so that current flows are kept to a minimum.

Appendix

BASIC DATA

Device	741C
Supply voltage range (+/−)	5 to 18V
Quiescent supply current	1.7mA
Gain/Bandwidth product·	1MHz
Slew-rate (V per μs)	0.5
Notes	Standard internally compensated operational amplifier

Device	748C
Supply voltage range (+/−)	5 to 18V
Quiescent supply current	1.7mA
Gain/Bandwidth product	1MHz
Slew-rate (V per μs)	0.5
Notes	Non-compensated 741C - bandwidth dependent on discrete compensation capacitor

Device	EL2001C
Supply voltage range (+/−)	5 to 15V
Quiescent supply current	1.3mA
Gain/Bandwidth product	70MHz
Slew-rate (V per μs)	200
Notes	High speed unity voltage gain buffer for video use, etc.

Device	NE5532
Supply voltage range (+/−)	3 to 20V
Quiescent supply current	10mA
Gain/Bandwidth product	10MHz
Slew-rate (V per μs)	9
Notes	Dual device, very low audio noise and distortion

Device	NE5534A
Supply voltage range (+/−)	3 to 20V
Quiescent supply current	4mA
Gain/Bandwidth product	10MHz
Slew-rate (V per μs)	13
Notes	Very low audio noise and distortion

Device	TLE2027C
Supply voltage range (+/−)	4 to 22V
Quiescent supply current	3.8mA
Gain/Bandwidth product	13MHz
Slew-rate (V per μs)	2.8
Notes	Very low audio noise and distortion

Device	TLE2037C
Supply voltage range (+/−)	4 to 22V
Quiescent supply current	3.8mA
Gain/Bandwidth product	76MHz
Slew-rate (V per μs)	7.5
Notes	Very low audio noise and distortion, internally compensated for voltage gains of 5x or more

Device	OP-77GP
Supply voltage range (+/−)	3 to 20V
Quiescent supply current	1.7mA
Gain/Bandwidth product	0.6MHz
Slew-rate (V per μs)	0.3
Notes	Low input offset voltage, very low noise at low frequencies, for precision d.c. applications

Device	CA3140E
Supply voltage range (+/−)	2 to 18V
Quiescent supply current	4mA
Gain/Bandwidth product	4.5MHz
Slew-rate (V per μs)	9
Notes	PMOS input stage, Class A output stage, suitable for single supply d.c. amplifiers

Device	CA3240E
Notes	Dual CA3140E

Device	LF351N
Supply voltage range (+/−)	5 to 18V
Quiescent supply current	1.8mA
Gain/Bandwidth product	4MHz
Slew-rate (V per μs)	13
Notes	Bifet device having Jfet input transistors, low audio distortion

Device	LF353N
Notes	Dual LF351N

Device	LF356N
Supply voltage range (+/−)	5 to 22V
Quiescent supply current	5mA
Gain/Bandwidth product	4.5MHz
Slew-rate (V per μs)	12
Notes	High performance Bifet device

Device	LM393N
Supply voltage range (+/−)	1 to 18V
Quiescent supply current	400μA
Response time	1.3μs
Notes	Dual voltage comparator for dual or single supply operation, open collector output stage (up to 50mA)

Please note we publish a vast range of Radio, Electronics and Computer books.

These should be available from all good Booksellers, Radio Component Dealers and Mail Order Companies.

However, should you experience difficulty in obtaining any title in your area, then please write directly to the Publisher enclosing payment to cover the cost of the book plus adequate postage.

If you would like a complete catalogue of our entire range of Radio, Electronics and Computer Books then please send a Stamped Addressed Envelope to:

BERNARD BABANI (publishing) LTD
THE GRAMPIANS
SHEPHERDS BUSH ROAD
LONDON W6 7NF
ENGLAND